The Ultimate Guide to Songwriting

Andrew Parry

Published by Andrew Parry, 2024.

THE ULTIMATE GUIDE TO SONGWRITING

First edition. October 11, 2024.

ISBN: 979-8227254405

Written by Andrew Parry.

Table of Contents

Inspiration: Finding the Spark for Your Song

Songwriting begins with a spark—a moment where an idea or emotion stirs within you and begs to be expressed through music. This initial burst of inspiration is often the most elusive part of the process, yet it's where the magic begins. Inspiration can come from just about anywhere: a personal experience, a conversation, a place, or even an emotion you're struggling to define. Finding that spark is less about waiting for it to arrive and more about opening yourself to it, creating the right environment for ideas to flourish.

Inspiration often strikes when you least expect it. It might be a phrase someone casually says that resonates with you, or a melody that comes to mind while you're driving, walking, or in the middle of a mundane task. Carrying a small notebook or using a notes app on your phone to capture these moments is essential. Inspiration doesn't follow a schedule, and if you don't capture it when it arrives, it might slip away. The same applies to melodies—sing or hum them into your phone's voice recorder the moment they pop into your head.

One of the most potent sources of inspiration for songwriters is personal experience. Songs that connect on a deep emotional level often come from an authentic place within the writer. Reflect on your life's highs and lows—joys, sorrows, triumphs, and failures. A relationship that has left a mark, a challenge you've overcome, or a dream you've chased can all fuel a song. Don't be afraid to tap into the rawest, most vulnerable parts of your life. These are the moments that, when transformed into music, resonate most strongly with listeners.

However, inspiration doesn't have to come from within. The world around you is full of stories waiting to be told. Read books, watch movies, listen to conversations, and immerse yourself in art. You'll often find that another person's experience can spark a creative idea of your own. This is not about copying; it's about allowing other stories to ignite your imagination. Often, a line from a movie or a scene from a novel can trigger an idea that you can transform into something uniquely your own.

Another fruitful way to find inspiration is to actively seek out new experiences. Travel to a new place, try a new activity, or learn something new. Stepping out of your routine can help break through creative blocks and introduce fresh ideas. Even simple changes in your daily routine, such as taking a different route to work or spending time in a new environment, can stimulate your creativity.

Nature can also be an incredible source of inspiration. There's something about being outdoors, surrounded by the rhythms and sounds of the natural world, that can free your mind from its usual constraints. A walk in the park, a trip to the beach, or even sitting quietly in your backyard can help reset your mental state and open you up to new ideas. The beauty and unpredictability of nature can often parallel the creative process itself, providing metaphors and imagery that can be transformed into lyrics and melodies.

WHILE INSPIRATION IS often spontaneous, it can also be nurtured by discipline. Many professional songwriters set aside specific times each day to write, whether they feel inspired or not. They treat songwriting like a muscle that needs regular exercise. By creating a routine and making space for creativity, you increase the likelihood of capturing moments of inspiration when they arise. You might not always write a hit song every time you sit down to create, but you'll be building the habit of showing up, and sometimes, that's when the spark hits.

Listening to other music is another critical way to fuel your creativity. Study the songs of artists you admire, and not just for their melodies or lyrics. Listen deeply to the structure, the way the verses lead into the chorus, the instrumentation, and the dynamics. Sometimes, just hearing a new chord progression or a particularly striking lyric can set your own creative gears in motion. You might find inspiration in a song's mood, its rhythm, or the way the artist expresses a particular emotion. It's not about imitating, but about seeing how other songwriters approach their craft and allowing that to feed into your own process.

Collaborating with other musicians can also open new doors of inspiration. When you work with someone else, you're exposed to their creative ideas, perspectives, and techniques. They might approach a melody or lyric in a way that you never would have considered, pushing you to think outside your usual patterns. Songwriting partnerships have sparked some of the greatest music in history, from Lennon and McCartney to Elton John and Bernie Taupin. A good collaborator challenges you and helps you explore new musical territory.

Finally, embrace the unpredictability of the creative process. Sometimes, inspiration comes in a flash and a song pours out in a matter of minutes. Other times, it might take weeks or months for an idea to fully form. Don't rush the process, and don't force it. Creativity ebbs and flows, and every songwriter's journey is different. Trust that if you remain open and actively engage in the world around you, the spark will find you.

Inspiration isn't about waiting for lightning to strike—it's about living with your eyes and ears open, staying curious, and being ready to capture ideas as they come. Whether it's a snippet of conversation, a melody you hear on the wind, or an emotion you've been carrying, your songs begin with that initial spark. By nurturing your creative environment and consistently showing up to the songwriting process, you'll be ready when inspiration finds you.

Crafting Compelling Lyrics

Writing lyrics is where a song truly comes to life. It's the part of songwriting that allows you to express emotions, tell stories, and connect with your audience on a deep, personal level. Crafting compelling lyrics can be both the most exciting and the most challenging part of the songwriting process. To create lyrics that resonate, it's essential to combine authenticity with technique, and inspiration with structure.

At its core, a great lyric communicates something real. Whether it's an emotion, an experience, or an observation, authenticity is what makes lyrics stand out. Listeners can tell when a songwriter is being genuine, and they can feel when the words come from a place of truth. This doesn't mean that every song has to be autobiographical, but it does mean that your lyrics should come from a place of emotional honesty. Even when writing fiction or fantasy-based songs, there should be an emotional truth that underpins your words.

One of the most effective ways to start writing lyrics is to focus on what you want to say. This can be a message, a feeling, or a story. Are you writing about love, heartbreak, self-discovery, or societal issues? Once you have a clear sense of what your song is about, the process of finding the right words becomes easier. Try jotting down key phrases, words, or images that come to mind when you think about your subject. This initial brainstorming session can help you zero in on the tone and themes of your song.

A useful tool for lyric writing is imagery. The old saying "show, don't tell" applies as much to songwriting as it does to other forms of writing. Instead of saying, "I'm sad," try painting a picture of sadness through vivid, specific details. Describing the feeling as "the rain falling against the window while the world turns gray" evokes an emotional response in the listener without explicitly stating the emotion. Using sensory details—sights, sounds, smells, and textures—can transport your audience into the moment you're describing.

Another aspect to consider is metaphor and simile. These literary devices can add layers of meaning to your lyrics. When you compare two things, you create connections between ideas that might not seem related at first glance. A well-placed metaphor can give your lyrics depth, making them more thought-provoking and memorable. For example, in Bob Dylan's *Blowin' in the Wind*, the wind is used as a metaphor for elusive answers to life's big questions. The lyric doesn't need to directly spell out the meaning, because the metaphor allows listeners to interpret it in a way that resonates with them.

When crafting lyrics, pay close attention to rhyme and rhythm. Lyrics are meant to be sung, so they need to flow smoothly when set to music. While not every line needs to rhyme, rhyme schemes can add a sense of structure and cohesion to your lyrics. Traditional rhyme schemes, such as ABAB or AABB, provide a familiar framework that listeners can easily follow, while internal rhymes (where words rhyme within a line rather than at the end) can add a subtle musicality to your lyrics. But be careful not to let rhyme dictate your content. It's important that your lyrics make sense and convey the intended emotion, rather than forcing a rhyme that feels awkward or out of place.

Rhythm is equally important. The way your lyrics are phrased—where the stresses fall and how syllables are emphasized—should complement the music. The rhythm of your lyrics should feel natural, aligning with the beats of the song and enhancing its overall groove. Experiment with phrasing by singing your lyrics over a melody or beat, adjusting words to ensure they flow smoothly with the music. Often, the placement of a word within a line can change the entire feel of the song, so don't be afraid to play around with different rhythmic patterns.

Another key element of lyric writing is structure. Most popular songs follow a standard format of verses, choruses, and sometimes a bridge. The verses typically tell the story or set up the theme, while the chorus drives home the main point or emotion of the song. The chorus is where your most memorable, singable lyrics usually live, so it's important to make these lines as impactful as possible. A well-crafted chorus will be both catchy and meaningful, leaving a lasting impression on the listener.

When it comes to writing verses, think about progression. Each verse should build upon the last, either deepening the story or exploring new facets of the theme. You don't want each verse to repeat the same idea with different words; instead, use them as opportunities to unfold the narrative or expand on the emotion. This keeps the listener engaged and invested in the journey your lyrics are taking them on.

Bridges offer another opportunity for creativity. The bridge typically provides a break from the established pattern of verse and chorus, often offering a new perspective or a shift in the emotional tone of the song. It's a chance to introduce a lyrical twist or a different musical idea before returning to the familiar refrain of the chorus. A well-placed bridge can elevate a song, adding an element of surprise and keeping the listener's attention.

Collaboration can also be incredibly helpful in the lyric-writing process. Sometimes, another songwriter can offer a fresh perspective on your words or suggest a line that you hadn't thought of. Don't be afraid to share your lyrics with others and ask for feedback. Often, an outside opinion can help you see your work in a new light and improve your lyrics in ways you might not have considered.

Ultimately, the most important thing in lyric writing is to stay true to your voice. Every songwriter has their own style, and what works for one person might not work for another. Some writers are more abstract, preferring to leave room for interpretation, while others are more direct, crafting clear narratives or messages. Both approaches are valid, and the key is to find what feels authentic to you. Trust your instincts and don't be afraid to take risks with your lyrics.

Song lyrics are more than just words set to music—they're a way to connect with your audience on an emotional level. Whether you're telling a story, expressing a feeling, or making a statement, your lyrics have the power to resonate with listeners and leave a lasting impression. By combining authenticity with technique, you can craft lyrics that not only sound good but also have real depth and meaning.

Developing Melodies That Stick

Melodies are the heart and soul of any song. They're what listeners hum long after the lyrics are forgotten, the core of what makes a piece of music memorable. Crafting a melody that not only fits your song but also sticks in people's minds requires a combination of creativity, intuition, and understanding of musical patterns. While inspiration plays a huge role, there are techniques and strategies you can use to develop melodies that resonate deeply with listeners.

At its essence, a melody is a series of notes played in a sequence that evokes an emotional response. The key to a strong melody is simplicity and repetition balanced with enough variation to keep it interesting. Many of the most iconic melodies, from the opening notes of *Let It Be* by The Beatles to the unmistakable melody in *Bohemian Rhapsody* by Queen, share a common trait: they are simple enough to be remembered but contain unique elements that make them stand out.

A great place to start when developing a melody is the chord progression of your song. Chords provide the harmonic foundation, and your melody should complement and enhance these chords. Play around with different note choices over your chords to see what fits. You'll often find that the most effective melodies use notes from the chord being played, particularly the root, third, and fifth notes of each chord. This creates a natural harmonic connection between the melody and the underlying music.

One of the most powerful tools in melody writing is the use of repetition. Repetition gives listeners something to latch onto, creating familiarity and a sense of structure. Think of how often you hear a melody repeat in a song's chorus—that repetition is what makes it stick. But the key is to use repetition wisely. If the melody repeats too much without any variation, it can become monotonous. The trick is to repeat enough to establish the melody but introduce subtle changes that keep it fresh. These variations could be slight changes in pitch, rhythm, or dynamics.

When crafting a melody, pay close attention to its shape or contour. Melody contour refers to the direction the notes move—whether they ascend, descend, or stay relatively flat. A well-constructed melody often has a distinct shape, such as starting low and rising to a peak before descending. This rise and fall create a sense of journey within the melody. You don't want your melody to feel static, so give it movement, allowing it to grow and recede in ways that enhance the emotion of the song. Melodies that rise during the chorus, for example, often feel more uplifting or intense, while descending melodies might evoke melancholy or resolution.

Rhythm is another crucial element of melody. A melody isn't just about which notes you choose, but also when and how those notes are delivered. Playing with rhythm can turn a simple melody into something that feels dynamic and engaging. Short, staccato notes create a different energy than long, sustained ones. Syncopation—where notes are played off the regular beat—can add a sense of tension or groove, making the melody more rhythmically interesting. Don't be afraid to experiment with different rhythms to see what works best for your song's mood.

One technique that can help generate new melodic ideas is improvisation. If you have a chord progression or rhythm already laid down, try singing or playing over it without worrying about structure or correctness. Let the melody come naturally, following where your ear takes you. Often, the best ideas come from these spontaneous moments. Record yourself while improvising so you can listen back and pick out any sections that stand out. Even if most of the improvisation isn't usable, you might find a small piece—a few notes or a phrase—that serves as the perfect foundation for your melody.

When you're developing your melody, consider the relationship between the verses, the chorus, and any other sections of the song. Verses usually have more room for exploration, allowing the melody to be more flexible and less repetitive, while the chorus typically features the most memorable, singable melody. The transition between these sections should feel natural, but each part should stand out in its own way. The chorus is where you want the melody to soar—it's the climax of your song's musical and emotional arc. Many successful songs feature a chorus melody that contrasts with the verse, creating a satisfying shift in energy when the chorus hits. It's also helpful to analyze melodies from songs that you admire. Take a closer look at how the melody interacts with the harmony, the rhythm, and the lyrics. How does the melody change between the verses and chorus? Does it repeat certain phrases or introduce new ideas? Pay attention to the contour of the melody—where it rises, falls, and stays steady. By studying the construction of other melodies, you can gain insight into techniques that you can apply to your own writing.

Creating a melody that sticks often comes down to balance. You want it to be memorable without being overly predictable, engaging without being too complex. One way to achieve this balance is by using motifs—small, repeating musical phrases that serve as the building blocks of your melody. A motif can be as simple as a three-note pattern that repeats throughout the song, with variations in pitch or rhythm. By developing a strong motif, you give listeners something familiar to hold onto, while still allowing room for the melody to evolve.

Another tool in your melodic toolkit is contrast. A melody that stays in the same register or follows the same rhythmic pattern throughout can become monotonous. Introduce contrast by varying the pitch range, using both high and low notes, or by changing the rhythmic feel from section to section. For example, if your verse melody is more laid-back and rhythmically loose, you might want to tighten up the rhythm in the chorus to create a sense of forward motion and excitement. Don't forget that lyrics and melody work hand in hand. Sometimes, the emotion or meaning of the lyrics can dictate the direction of the melody. A lyric that expresses longing might be best served by a melody that climbs upward, while a lyric about loss might naturally descend. As you write your melody, think about how it aligns with the message and emotion of the words. In the end, the best melodies are those that feel like they belong to the song—they flow naturally and complement the other elements, whether it's the chords, the lyrics, or the rhythm. Developing melodies that stick isn't about following a strict formula, but rather about trusting your ear, experimenting, and refining your ideas until they feel right.

Melody is where the emotional impact of a song often lies, and it's the part that will stay with listeners long after the song is over. By combining intuition, technical skill, and creativity, you can craft melodies that leave a lasting impression.

Building Chord Progressions that Support Your Song

Chord progressions are the backbone of any song, providing the harmonic structure that underpins the melody and lyrics. A well-crafted chord progression not only enhances the emotional impact of your song but also gives it a sense of direction and movement. While melody and lyrics often grab the listener's attention, it's the chord progression that gives the song its foundation, creating the mood and supporting the story you're telling.

At its most basic, a chord progression is a sequence of chords played in a specific order. Each chord is built from notes in a particular key, and the way these chords are arranged can create different emotional effects. The key to building a strong chord progression is understanding how chords relate to one another and how they can be used to evoke different feelings—whether it's tension, resolution, joy, or melancholy.

The most common and accessible chord progressions are built using the chords of a major or minor scale. In any given key, there are seven basic chords, each corresponding to one of the notes in the scale. For example, in the key of C major, the chords are: C major (I), D minor (ii), E minor (iii), F major (IV), G major (V), A minor (vi), and B diminished (vii°). The Roman numerals represent the position of each chord in the scale, with uppercase for major chords and lowercase for minor chords. These chords are the building blocks of your progression, and their relationships with each other form the harmonic landscape of your song.

One of the most popular chord progressions in modern music is the I-IV-V progression. In the key of C, this would be C major, F major, and G major. This progression is so common because it provides a strong sense of movement, with the V chord (G major) creating tension that resolves back to the I chord (C major). The I-IV-V progression is used in countless songs across genres, from pop and rock to blues and folk, because it feels familiar and satisfying to the listener.

Another widely used progression is the I-V-vi-IV progression, which is incredibly versatile and has been the backbone of many hit songs. In the key of C, this progression would be C major, G major, A minor, and F major. This progression has a more emotional or bittersweet feel, often associated with love songs or ballads. The movement from the major I and V chords to the minor vi chord adds a touch of melancholy before resolving on the IV chord, which gives the progression a sense of completion.

When building a chord progression, think about the emotional tone you want to convey. Major chords tend to sound bright and uplifting, while minor chords evoke a more introspective or somber mood. By mixing major and minor chords in different sequences, you can create a wide range of emotional effects. For instance, a progression that begins with a major chord and moves to a minor chord can introduce an unexpected shift in mood, creating tension or a sense of longing. It's also important to consider the function of each chord in your progression.

Some chords create a feeling of stability, while others create tension that needs to be resolved. The I chord (the tonic) is the most stable chord in any key, providing a sense of home. The V chord (the dominant) creates tension and is often used to lead back to the I chord, providing resolution. The IV chord (the subdominant) sits between these two, offering a transition that feels neither fully tense nor fully resolved. By understanding the roles of these chords, you can craft progressions that lead the listener on a satisfying harmonic journey.

Don't be afraid to experiment with chord substitutions or inversions to add interest to your progression. For example, instead of playing a plain C major chord, you might try a Cmaj7 chord, which adds a richer, more complex sound.

Inversions, where you play the same chord but with a different note in the bass, can also change the flavor of a progression. These subtle changes can give your song a more distinctive sound without altering its basic structure.

Another powerful technique is to use a secondary dominant chord. In a standard I-IV-V progression, the V chord naturally resolves to the I chord. But you can add more tension and excitement by introducing a dominant chord that leads into the IV or vi chord. For example, in the key of C major, instead of going straight from C major to F major, you could introduce a D7 chord (the dominant of G major) before landing on G major, which then leads back to C major. This creates a more dynamic harmonic progression, adding color and movement to your song.

While it's important to understand these theoretical concepts, building chord progressions is also about intuition. Sometimes the most effective progressions come from simply experimenting on your instrument, trying different combinations of chords until something feels right. Don't be afraid to step outside the conventional progressions and trust your ear. Music theory is a guide, but it's your creativity that drives the process.

Rhythm plays a crucial role in how your chord progression feels. The same set of chords can sound completely different depending on how they're played. A progression that moves quickly from one chord to the next might create a sense of urgency or excitement, while holding on a chord for several bars can build tension or create a laid-back, reflective mood. Experiment with different rhythmic patterns—strumming, fingerpicking, or using syncopated rhythms—to see how they affect the feel of your progression.

One way to keep your chord progression fresh and engaging is to introduce a key change or modulation. Modulating to a different key can bring a new energy to the song, especially in the bridge or final chorus. It creates a sense of lifting or expanding the emotional palette of the song. Even a temporary shift to a related key (like moving from C major to A minor) can add depth and complexity to your progression. It's also important to consider how your chord progression interacts with your melody. A strong progression supports the melody, allowing it to shine, while also creating a harmonic backdrop that enhances the emotional impact of the song. When you're developing a melody, try singing or playing over different chord progressions to see how the two elements fit together. You might find that adjusting a chord—or even switching to a different key—can make your melody more effective.

Finally, building chord progressions is an ongoing learning process. The more songs you write, the more you'll develop your instinct for what works. Study the progressions in songs you love—figure out what chords are being used and why they work so well. With time and practice, you'll start to see patterns and develop your own approach to building progressions that serve your song's unique mood and message. In the end, a chord progression's role is to support your song's overall emotional arc. Whether simple or complex, predictable or surprising, it's the harmonic structure that holds your song together. By experimenting with different combinations, trusting your ear, and understanding the emotional power of chords, you'll be able to build progressions that not only support but elevate your music.

Analyzing Popular Songs for Songwriting Techniques

One of the most effective ways to improve your own songwriting is by studying and analyzing the techniques used in popular songs. These songs have stood the test of time or captured the attention of a wide audience, often because they employ songwriting strategies that are both creative and accessible. By dissecting these songs, you can uncover the tools and methods that made them successful and apply those techniques to your own music.

To begin your analysis, start by choosing songs that resonate with you or that are considered classics within their genre. Whether it's the timeless appeal of a Beatles track or the emotional depth of a ballad by Adele, each song can offer valuable insights into different aspects of songwriting—melody, harmony, lyrics, structure, and more. Listening with a critical ear and taking notes on what works in each song will help you internalize these techniques.

The first element to pay attention to is **song structure**. Most popular songs follow a relatively predictable format, such as verse-chorus-verse-chorus-bridge-chorus, but the way this structure is handled can vary widely. Look at how each section functions within the song. What does the verse establish? How does the chorus deliver a memorable hook? What role does the bridge play in shifting the mood or introducing new ideas? The interplay between verses, choruses, and bridges is crucial in creating the ebb and flow that keeps listeners engaged. Pay attention to how the song builds or evolves over time—how it starts, where it peaks, and how it resolves.

For example, take The Beatles' classic *Hey Jude*. The song begins with a simple piano melody and Paul McCartney's soothing vocals, but as it progresses, more instruments are introduced, and the emotion intensifies. The verses lead into a powerful, sing-along chorus, and then the song takes a surprising turn in the coda, with its extended "na-na-na" section. This shift in structure creates a lasting emotional impact and gives the song its unique character. Notice how the chorus in *Hey Jude* isn't just a repetition of the same idea—it builds in intensity each time, taking the listener on a dynamic emotional journey.

Next, focus on **melody**. Popular songs often feature melodies that are both simple and catchy, yet contain enough variation to avoid becoming monotonous. Analyze how the melody flows—does it rise and fall in an interesting way? Does it have moments of repetition and moments of contrast? A melody that moves smoothly between the verses and the chorus often feels natural, while a sharp contrast in the chorus can create an exciting shift that grabs the listener's attention.

A great example of this is in Whitney Houston's *I Will Always Love You*. The verses are relatively understated, allowing her voice to deliver the emotion with minimal accompaniment. But when the chorus hits, the melody soars, with Whitney's powerful vocals reaching a peak that adds an undeniable sense of drama. This contrast between the restrained verses and the explosive chorus makes the melody unforgettable and enhances the song's emotional punch.

Lyrics are another crucial aspect of popular songs that deserve close examination. Compelling lyrics often strike a balance between being relatable and poetic. They may tell a story, express a personal emotion, or tap into universal themes like love, loss, or self-discovery. Pay attention to the **language** used—how does the songwriter evoke specific emotions or imagery through word choice? Are the lyrics direct, or do they leave room for interpretation?

Consider Bob Dylan's *The Times They Are A-Changin'*, which masterfully combines simplicity with depth. The lyrics speak to social change and revolution, using plain language that anyone can understand, but the message resonates on a profound level. The repetition of the title line at the end of each verse drives home the theme of inevitability and progress, making the song not just a commentary on its time, but a timeless anthem for change. Dylan's ability to craft lyrics that feel both personal and universal is part of what makes his songs so enduring.Don't overlook the **harmonic structure** of the songs you analyze. Chord progressions form the foundation of most popular songs, and understanding how they work can provide insight into why certain progressions are so effective. Some songs use simple progressions like I-IV-V or I-V-vi-IV, but it's how the progression interacts wi th the melody and lyrics that gives the song its emotional power.

For example, the I-V-vi-IV progression has been used in countless hits, from *Let It Be* by The Beatles to *With or Without You* by U2. This progression has a built-in emotional arc, moving from the major chords to the relative minor (vi), creating a bittersweet feeling that resonates with listeners. Analyzing how different songs use this same progression in unique ways can teach you how to work within familiar frameworks while still maintaining originality. In addition to the core elements of melody, harmony, and lyrics, pay attention to the **dynamics** in popular songs. Dynamics refer to how the intensity of the music changes over the course of the song. These changes—whether subtle or dramatic—help to keep the listener engaged. A song that builds gradually, introducing new layers of sound or increasing in volume and energy, can create a powerful emotional payoff. On the other hand, a song that alternates between quiet and loud sections can create tension and release, which is equally effective.

A great example of dynamic use is *Smells Like Teen Spirit* by Nirvana. The song's quiet verses, where Kurt Cobain's voice is almost a murmur, contrast sharply with the explosive, distortion-heavy chorus. This stark dynamic shift heightens the intensity of the song and reflects the raw, rebellious energy that defined the grunge movement. By paying attention to how dynamics are used in your favorite songs, you can learn how to manipulate volume and intensity to enhance the emotional impact of your own work.

Rhythm is another area that deserves close attention. Popular songs often feature rhythms that are easy to follow but may include subtle variations or syncopations that keep the listener interested. Look at how rhythm interacts with both the melody and lyrics. Is the rhythm driving the song forward, creating a sense of urgency, or is it more laid-back, allowing the melody to take center stage? Songs like *Billie Jean* by Michael Jackson have iconic rhythms that not only drive the song but also become a central part of its identity.

Finally, consider the **production** of the song. While songwriting and production are different skill sets, the way a song is arranged and produced can have a huge impact on how it's received. Analyze how instruments are layered, how effects like reverb or delay are used, and how the mix emphasizes certain elements. Even if you're primarily focused on songwriting, understanding how production techniques can enhance a song will give you a better sense of how to present your music in the best possible light.

The Power of Melody: Creating Memorable Tunes

Melody is the soul of a song, the element that grabs the listener's attention and sticks in their memory long after the song has ended. A strong melody has the power to evoke emotions, tell stories, and resonate with people on a deep, instinctual level. Whether it's the soaring chorus of a power ballad or the infectious hook of a pop song, melody is often what makes a song memorable and distinctive.

But what exactly makes a melody stick? The answer lies in a combination of simplicity, repetition, variation, and emotional connection. These elements work together to create a tune that is not only pleasing to the ear but also has lasting emotional impact. Crafting a memorable melody involves finding a balance between familiarity and surprise, predictability and innovation.

At the heart of most great melodies is **simplicity**. Simplicity doesn't mean boring or basic—it means creating a melody that is easy to grasp and hum along to. Some of the most iconic melodies in music history are remarkably simple, yet they resonate deeply with listeners. Think about the opening notes of Beethoven's *Ode to Joy* or Paul McCartney's *Let It Be*. These melodies are built around just a few notes and yet evoke a profound emotional response. Simple melodies are more likely to be remembered because they don't overwhelm the listener with complexity. Instead, they invite participation—listeners can easily sing along, hum the tune, or recall it later.

Repetition is another key component of memorable melodies. Our brains are wired to recognize and remember patterns, so when a melody repeats itself within a song, it becomes familiar and easier to retain. This is why choruses in popular music often feature a repeated melody—the repetition reinforces the tune in the listener's mind. However, repetition alone isn't enough. If a melody repeats without any variation, it risks becoming monotonous. The challenge is to find ways to repeat the melody while keeping it fresh.

Variation is what keeps a melody interesting. Even small changes—a note that's slightly higher or lower, a rhythmic alteration, or a shift in dynamics—can prevent a melody from becoming too predictable. Many successful melodies repeat with subtle differences that maintain the listener's interest while still providing the comfort of familiarity. For instance, in Adele's *Someone Like You*, the verses and choruses repeat the same basic melody, but there are slight shifts in rhythm and dynamics that give each section its own emotional flavor. This balance of repetition and variation creates a melody that feels both grounded and dynamic.

A memorable melody often follows a natural **contour**—a rise and fall that mimics the way we speak or express emotions. Think of a melody as a journey. It might start at a low point, climb to a peak, and then descend again. This contour creates a sense of movement and progression, which keeps the listener engaged. Melodies that stay at the same pitch for too long can feel static, while melodies with too much movement can feel chaotic. Finding a balance between upward and downward motion in your melody creates a sense of flow and emotional direction.

When crafting a melody, consider the **intervals** between notes. Melodies that are too jumpy, with large leaps between notes, can feel disjointed and difficult to follow. On the other hand, melodies that move by small, stepwise intervals often feel smoother and more natural. Many memorable melodies feature a combination of small steps and occasional larger leaps. For example, *Somewhere Over the Rainbow* famously opens with an octave leap, a large interval that instantly grabs the listener's attention, before settling into smaller steps that give the melody its flowing, dreamlike quality.

The **rhythm** of a melody is just as important as the notes themselves. A melody's rhythm can determine whether it feels energetic, laid-back, tense, or relaxed. By playing with rhythmic patterns, you can shape the overall feel of the melody. Syncopation—placing accents on offbeats—can create a sense of urgency or groove, while long, sustained notes can evoke a more contemplative mood. Michael Jackson's *Billie Jean* is a great example of how rhythm can drive a melody. The rhythm of the vocal melody, with its syncopated phrasing, plays off the relentless beat of the bassline, creating a tension that propels the song forward.

Another essential aspect of crafting a memorable melody is its **emotional connection**. A melody that resonates with listeners isn't just catchy—it also taps into their emotions. Whether it's the haunting beauty of a minor-key melody in a ballad or the triumphant energy of a major-key anthem, the emotional tone of your melody should align with the overall mood of your song. One of the most powerful tools in a songwriter's arsenal is **melodic contrast**. A melody that contrasts sharply with the harmony or lyrics can create a profound emotional effect. For instance, a sad lyric paired with a major-key melody can create a sense of bitter-sweetness, as heard in songs like The Smiths' *There Is a Light That Never Goes Out*. The bright melody contrasts with the dark, melancholy lyrics, creating an emotional complexity that makes the song more impactful.

Additionally, **melodic motifs**—short, repeating musical phrases—can serve as the foundation for a memorable melody. These motifs are the building blocks of your tune, providing a recognizable pattern that listeners can latch onto. A motif doesn't have to be complex; it could be as simple as a three-note phrase that repeats throughout the song. By developing and evolving your motif, you can create a melody that feels cohesive and well-structured.

It's also important to remember that melody and **harmony** are deeply intertwined. A melody that works beautifully over one chord progression might feel awkward or dissonant over another. When developing your melody, think about how it interacts with the chords beneath it. Strong melodies often emphasize notes that are part of the underlying chord, creating a sense of consonance and harmony. At the same time, a well-placed dissonance—a note that isn't part of the chord—can add tension and drama, especially if it resolves to a more stable note.

When it comes to melody, it's not just about the notes you choose but also about the **space** between them. Sometimes, the most effective melodies are the ones that leave room for silence. Pausing between phrases or leaving gaps in your melody can create a sense of anticipation, giving listeners time to absorb the music before moving on to the next phrase. These moments of rest can also enhance the emotional impact of the notes that follow, making the melody feel more dynamic and expressive.

Analyzing successful melodies from a variety of genres can offer valuable insight into how different songwriters approach the craft. Look at how artists like Paul McCartney, Stevie Wonder, or Taylor Swift use melody to shape their songs. What makes their melodies stand out? How do they use repetition, variation, and contour to create tunes that stick in your head? By studying these techniques, you can start to develop your own melodic style.

Ultimately, creating memorable melodies is about finding a balance between instinct and technique. While music theory can offer guidelines and tools for crafting melodies, some of the most iconic tunes have come from songwriters following their gut, allowing inspiration to guide their choices. Trust your ear, experiment with different ideas, and don't be afraid to take risks. Sometimes, the most memorable melodies are the ones that break the rules.

At the end of the day, the power of melody lies in its ability to connect with people on a fundamental, emotional level. Whether it's a simple, singable hook or a complex, winding tune, a strong melody has the power to move listeners and make your song unforgettable. By combining creativity with technique, you can craft melodies that not only stick in people's minds but also touch their hearts.

Rhythm: The Pulse of Your Song

Rhythm is the driving force behind every song, the invisible pulse that gives a track its energy and momentum. It is what makes us tap our feet, nod our heads, or sway to the beat without even thinking. While melody and harmony might grab the spotlight, rhythm provides the framework that holds everything together. In songwriting, rhythm is about more than just keeping time—it's about how the music feels, how it moves, and how it connects with the listener on a physical and emotional level.

At its core, rhythm is the pattern of sounds and silences in a song. It's the way notes are arranged over time, creating a sense of forward motion. Rhythm can be simple or complex, steady or syncopated, but it always plays a crucial role in shaping the overall feel of your song. The choice of rhythm can change the mood, intensity, and style of a song, making it one of the most powerful tools in a songwriter's arsenal.

When thinking about rhythm, the first thing to consider is **tempo**, or the speed at which your song moves. Tempo sets the pace for everything that happens in your song. A slow, steady tempo might give your song a laid-back, reflective feel, while a faster tempo creates excitement and urgency. The same chord progression or melody can feel entirely different depending on the tempo. For example, a ballad like *Let It Be* by The Beatles has a slow, deliberate tempo that invites introspection, while a fast-paced song like *Good Times Bad Times* by Led Zeppelin creates a sense of drive and energy. When crafting a song, choosing the right tempo can make all the difference in how your song is perceived and experienced.

Beyond tempo, the **time signature** of a song plays a major role in shaping its rhythm. Most popular music is written in 4/4 time, meaning there are four beats in each measure, with the quarter note getting the beat. This is the most familiar and comfortable time signature for listeners, which is why it's so common in genres like rock, pop, and hip-hop. However, experimenting with other time signatures can add a unique rhythmic flavor to your music. For instance, 3/4 or 6/8 time, often found in waltzes or folk music, gives a song a lilting, swaying quality, while an odd time signature like 5/4 or 7/8 can create a sense of tension or unpredictability, as heard in songs like *Take Five* by Dave Brubeck or *Money* by Pink Floyd.

The **beat** is the basic unit of rhythm, the regular pulse that listeners latch onto. In many genres, the beat is emphasized by the drums or bass, giving the song its groove. But rhythm in songwriting goes beyond just the beat itself—what really brings rhythm to life is the way different elements interact with that beat. In a song, the rhythm of the melody, the rhythm of the accompaniment, and the rhythm of the percussion all work together to create the overall rhythmic texture.

ONE OF THE MOST EFFECTIVE ways to add interest and complexity to your rhythm is through **syncopation**. Syncopation occurs when you place accents or stress on offbeats or unexpected parts of the rhythm, creating a sense of surprise and forward motion. It's a common feature in many genres, from jazz to reggae to pop. Syncopation breaks up the monotony of a straightforward beat, giving the rhythm a more dynamic, unpredictable feel. Michael Jackson's *Billie Jean* is a great example of how syncopation can add an infectious groove to a song. The rhythmic placement of the bass line and vocal phrases on the offbeat creates a sense of tension and release, making the song feel irresistibly danceable.

Groove is another critical aspect of rhythm, especially in genres like funk, hip-hop, and R&B. Groove refers to the way all the rhythmic elements in a song come together to create a compelling, cohesive feel. It's the interaction between the drums, bass, guitar, and other instruments that gives the song its momentum and makes it feel "in the pocket." A tight, well-executed groove can make even a simple chord progression come alive, while a loose or inconsistent groove can make a song feel disjointed. The funk classic *Superstition* by Stevie Wonder is a masterclass in groove. Every element of the rhythm section locks together perfectly, creating a deep, infectious groove that drives the entire song.

When crafting the rhythm for your song, don't forget the power of **space**. Silence, or the absence of sound, is just as important as the notes themselves. Leaving space in your rhythm—whether it's a pause between phrases or a sudden drop in the beat—creates a sense of tension and anticipation. The space between notes can make the rhythm feel more dynamic and can heighten the impact when the music kicks back in. Think of how a song like *In the Air Tonight* by Phil Collins uses silence and space in the verses to build suspense, leading up to the famous drum break. The use of silence makes the eventual return of the rhythm all the more powerful.

Rhythm can also be used to convey **emotion**. A slow, steady rhythm might evoke a sense of calm or sadness, while a fast, driving rhythm can create excitement or urgency. By varying the rhythm within a song, you can take the listener on an emotional journey. For example, a song might start with a slow, gentle rhythm in the verses, only to shift to a faster, more energetic rhythm in the chorus, creating a sense of contrast and release. A great example of this is in Queen's *Bohemian Rhapsody*, where the song transitions between several different rhythmic feels, from the slow, ballad-like intro to the fast, operatic middle section. This rhythmic variation mirrors the dramatic shifts in the song's narrative and emotional tone.

Another important aspect of rhythm is how it interacts with **lyrics and melody**. The rhythm of your lyrics—how the words are phrased and where the syllables fall in relation to the beat—can have a huge impact on the overall feel of your song. You might choose to align the rhythm of the melody closely with the beat for a straightforward, driving feel, or you might experiment with more complex phrasing, where the melody floats above or around the beat, creating a sense of freedom or syncopation. Rappers, for example, often play with the rhythm of their lyrics, using complex internal rhymes and offbeat phrasing to create rhythmic tension and excitement, as seen in songs by artists like Kendrick Lamar or Eminem.

Instrumentation also plays a key role in shaping rhythm. Different instruments bring different rhythmic textures to a song. Percussion instruments like drums and tambourines provide a clear, driving beat, while guitars, pianos, and bass can add syncopation, groove, or rhythmic embellishments. Even vocals can be treated as a rhythmic instrument, especially in genres like hip-hop or pop, where vocal delivery often has a percussive quality. By layering different rhythmic elements from various instruments, you can create a rich, complex rhythmic texture that enhances the overall feel of your song.

As you develop the rhythm for your song, it's important to consider how the rhythm **evolves** over the course of the track. Does the rhythm stay consistent throughout, or does it change in different sections of the song? Varying the rhythm between the verse, chorus, and bridge can help maintain the listener's interest and give each section its own distinct feel. For example, the verses might have a laid-back, syncopated groove, while the chorus features a more straightforward, driving rhythm that feels like a release of energy. This contrast helps to create a sense of progression and keeps the listener engaged.

In the end, rhythm is the pulse of your song—it's what gives your music life and movement. Whether you're writing a simple, acoustic ballad or a complex, groove-heavy funk track, the rhythm you choose will shape the listener's experience of the song. By experimenting with tempo, time signature, syncopation, and groove, and by paying attention to how rhythm interacts with melody and lyrics, you can create a rhythmic foundation that not only supports your song but elevates it to new heights.

Rhythm is where music meets the body. It's what makes us move, feel, and connect with the song on a physical level. When you tap into the power of rhythm, you tap into the core of what makes music so universally engaging and emotionally powerful.

Exploring Harmony: Adding Depth and Emotion

Harmony is the secret ingredient that brings depth and richness to a song. While melody often takes the spotlight, harmony is the supporting actor that adds emotional weight and complexity. Harmony gives music its layers, its sense of space, and its ability to evoke a range of emotions, from warmth and serenity to tension and resolution. Understanding how to use harmony effectively can transform a simple melody into something more profound and emotionally resonant.

At its most basic level, harmony occurs when two or more notes are played simultaneously, creating a chord. The relationship between these notes determines the color and emotional tone of the harmony. Some chords feel bright and uplifting, while others evoke sadness, tension, or ambiguity. By choosing different combinations of notes, you can craft harmonies that align with the mood of your song and enhance the message you're trying to convey.

To begin exploring harmony, it's helpful to understand how chords are built. Chords are typically made up of three or more notes played together. The most common type of chord is the **triad**, which consists of three notes: the root, the third, and the fifth. The root is the foundation of the chord, the third determines whether the chord is major (happy, bright) or minor (sad, moody), and the fifth adds stability. For example, in the key of C major, a C major triad consists of the notes C (root), E (third), and G (fifth). If you lower the third to an E flat, you get a C minor chord, which has a darker, more melancholic feel.

Major and minor chords are the building blocks of harmony, but there's much more to explore. **Seventh chords**, for example, add an extra layer of complexity by including a fourth note—the seventh. In a C major seventh chord (Cmaj7), the notes are C, E, G, and B. This chord has a lush, jazzy quality that adds sophistication to your harmony. On the other hand, a **dominant seventh chord** (like G7 in the key of C) creates a sense of tension that begs for resolution, often leading back to the tonic chord (C major). This tension and release are essential elements of Western harmony and can be used to give your music a sense of direction and movement.

Dissonance is another important concept in harmony. Dissonance occurs when notes clash, creating tension that seeks resolution. While dissonance can sound jarring, it can also add emotional intensity to a song. By resolving dissonant chords to more stable, consonant chords, you can create a feeling of release and satisfaction. This tension and resolution are fundamental to harmony, allowing you to control the emotional ebb and flow of your song. For example, in a standard blues progression, the dominant seventh chord (G7 in the key of C) introduces dissonance that resolves back to the tonic chord (C), creating a satisfying sense of closure.

ONE OF THE MOST POWERFUL tools in harmony is the concept of **chord progressions**. A chord progression is simply a series of chords played in a specific order. The way these chords move from one to the next can evoke different emotional responses. Some progressions feel stable and predictable, while others create a sense of surprise or tension. A simple yet effective chord progression is the I-IV-V progression, where the chords are built on the first, fourth, and fifth degrees of the scale. In the key of C, this would be C (I), F (IV), and G (V). This progression has been the backbone of countless pop, rock, and folk songs because it feels natural and satisfying.

More complex progressions, such as the I-V-vi-IV progression (C-G-Am-F in the key of C), introduce minor chords, which add emotional depth. The use of a minor chord in an otherwise major progression can create a bittersweet, reflective tone, which is why this progression is so common in love songs and ballads. The minor vi chord introduces a touch of sadness or longing, which contrasts with the brightness of the major I, IV, and V chords, giving the progression emotional complexity.

Voice leading is another important aspect of harmony that can add sophistication to your chord progressions. Voice leading refers to the smooth movement of individual notes (or voices) from one chord to the next. Instead of jumping between chords in a blocky way, voice leading ensures that each note in the chord moves by the smallest possible interval, creating a seamless transition between harmonies. For example, in a progression from C major (C-E-G) to G major (G-B-D), the note G stays the same, while E moves up to G and C moves up to B. This creates a smooth, connected feel between the two chords, which can make your harmony sound more polished and natural.

To deepen your exploration of harmony, try experimenting with **inversions**. Inversions occur when you change the order of notes in a chord, placing a note other than the root in the bass. For example, in a C major chord, you could play the E as the lowest note instead of the C, creating what's called the first inversion (C/E). This doesn't change the basic harmonic function of the chord, but it adds a different texture and color. Inversions can create smoother transitions between chords and add variety to your harmony without altering the underlying progression.

Another way to add depth to your harmony is through **modal interchange**. This involves borrowing chords from parallel modes (scales with the same root note but different qualities). For instance, if you're writing in the key of C major, you might borrow a chord from C minor, such as the iv chord (Fm). This creates a surprising shift in mood, adding emotional richness to your harmony. The contrast between the major and minor modes can evoke feelings of tension, mystery, or melancholy, depending on how it's used. The Beatles often employed modal interchange in their songs to add harmonic interest and complexity.

HARMONY ALSO EXTENDS beyond chords and into **vocal harmonies**, where multiple voices sing different notes simultaneously to create a rich, layered sound. Vocal harmonies can elevate a melody, adding warmth and depth. In many classic rock and pop songs, vocal harmonies are a signature element. Think of the lush harmonies in The Beach Boys' *Good Vibrations* or The Eagles' *Hotel California*. These harmonies don't just support the melody—they enhance it, adding emotional resonance and making the song more memorable. Even simple harmonies, like singing a third or a fifth above the main melody, can add a powerful sense of fullness to your song.

As you explore harmony, consider how it interacts with **melody**. A strong melody often highlights the most important notes of the underlying chords, creating a sense of unity between the melody and the harmony. However, experimenting with harmonies that contrast or even clash with the melody can create moments of tension and intrigue. This technique is often used in jazz, where the melody might play one note while the harmony introduces dissonant chords underneath, creating a complex, layered sound.

Finally, harmony is about **emotion**. The chords you choose and how you arrange them have a direct impact on how your song feels. A song with mostly major chords will likely feel bright, optimistic, or triumphant, while a song that leans into minor or diminished chords might evoke sadness, tension, or mystery. By carefully selecting your harmonies, you can guide the listener's emotional journey, amplifying the message of your lyrics and the mood of your melody.

In the end, harmony is about adding depth and dimension to your music. Whether you're using simple triads, rich seventh chords, or complex dissonances, harmony is the key to creating a full, emotionally engaging sound. As you continue to experiment with different harmonic techniques, you'll discover new ways to enhance your songs and evoke powerful emotional responses from your listeners. By mastering harmony, you unlock the ability to add layers of meaning and beauty to your music, transforming simple melodies into deeply resonant compositions.

Dynamics: Playing with Volume and Intensity

Dynamics are the secret weapon in songwriting, often overlooked but immensely powerful in shaping the emotional impact of a song. By controlling volume and intensity, dynamics allow you to create contrast, build tension, and release energy, all of which can turn a simple melody into a moving, dramatic experience. From the softest whisper to the loudest roar, the way you manipulate dynamics can make the difference between a song that feels flat and one that takes the listener on an emotional journey.

In music, dynamics refer to variations in volume and intensity. It's not just about loud versus soft—it's about how you transition between those extremes and how you use them to underscore the emotional arc of a song. Dynamics can be used to emphasize certain parts of the song, guide the listener's attention, or create moments of surprise. They are a tool for storytelling, allowing you to amplify the emotions of your lyrics and melody through changes in how the music is delivered.

One of the most common dynamic techniques is **contrast**—shifting between loud and soft sections to create a sense of drama and tension. Many classic songs use this technique to great effect. For example, Nirvana's *Smells Like Teen Spirit* alternates between soft, subdued verses and loud, explosive choruses. The quiet verses draw the listener in, creating a sense of anticipation, and when the chorus hits, the sudden increase in volume releases all the pent-up energy. This dynamic contrast is what makes the song feel so powerful and engaging. The quiet moments give the loud moments more impact, and the loud moments make the quiet ones more intimate.

Crescendos and **decrescendos** are another important dynamic tool. A crescendo is a gradual increase in volume, while a decrescendo (or diminuendo) is a gradual decrease. These dynamic shifts can build excitement and tension or bring a sense of calm and resolution. A well-placed crescendo can create the feeling of an emotional climax in a song, while a decrescendo can bring the listener back down to a more reflective or contemplative space.

A great example of a crescendo in action is *Fix You* by Coldplay. The song begins quietly, with just vocals and organ, creating a soft, introspective mood. As the song progresses, more instruments are introduced, and the volume gradually increases until it reaches a powerful crescendo in the final chorus. This dynamic build mirrors the emotional journey of the lyrics, amplifying the feelings of hope and redemption. The crescendo feels like a cathartic release, making the song's conclusion feel even more impactful.

Sudden shifts in dynamics can also be used for dramatic effect. These shifts—known as **terraced dynamics**—involve moving from loud to soft or vice versa without a gradual transition. This technique can create moments of surprise, keeping the listener on their toes. In *Bohemian Rhapsody* by Queen, for example, there are moments where the music shifts abruptly from soft, ballad-like sections to loud, operatic segments. These sudden changes in volume add to the theatrical quality of the song and keep the listener engaged by breaking the expectations of a traditional song structure.

Dynamics are not just about loud versus soft—they are also about **intensity**. You can play a part of the song softly but with great intensity, or you can play it loudly but with a more relaxed feel. Intensity refers to the emotional weight behind the notes, and it's a key factor in creating dynamics. A song can feel intense without being loud, simply by the way the instruments or vocals are delivered. For example, the verse of a song might be sung quietly, but with emotional intensity that keeps the listener hooked. In contrast, the chorus might be louder but more celebratory, creating a release of that tension.

One of the simplest but most effective ways to use dynamics is through **layering instruments**. By adding or subtracting layers of sound, you can create a dynamic build or breakdown without changing the volume directly. For example, starting a song with just a solo acoustic guitar and gradually introducing drums, bass, and other instruments can create a natural crescendo as the song progresses. Conversely, stripping the arrangement down to just vocals and one instrument for a verse or bridge can create a dynamic dip that draws the listener in. A perfect example of this can be found in *With or Without You* by U2, where the gradual introduction of new instrumental layers creates a dynamic build that culminates in an emotionally charged climax.

Vocals are another area where dynamics play a crucial role. **Vocal dynamics** can add depth and emotional nuance to a song. By shifting from a soft, breathy tone in the verses to a more powerful, full-voiced delivery in the chorus, you can create a dynamic contrast that highlights the emotional content of the lyrics. In *Rolling in the Deep* by Adele, the verses are sung with restraint, almost as if holding back the full emotional force, but when the chorus hits, the vocal intensity ramps up, delivering a powerful punch that makes the chorus feel like an emotional explosion.

Rhythmic dynamics are another way to create contrast and intensity. Even if the volume of the music stays the same, the intensity can be heightened or softened by changing the rhythmic feel. Playing more aggressively with a driving rhythm can make a song feel more intense, while pulling back on the rhythm, using more space between notes, can create a more relaxed or contemplative feel. A song like *Take Five* by The Dave Brubeck Quartet uses rhythmic dynamics to keep the listener engaged, even though the overall volume of the track remains fairly constant. The syncopation and use of off-beats create dynamic tension that keeps the rhythm feeling fresh and exciting.

Incorporating dynamics into your songwriting doesn't just happen at the macro level, with changes from verse to chorus or verse to bridge. **Micro-dynamics**—subtle variations in volume or intensity within a phrase or even a single note—can add a great deal of emotional depth to a performance. A singer might start a note softly and then swell into it, or a guitarist might strike a chord gently and let it build in intensity. These small shifts in dynamics can add nuance and expression to your music, making it feel more human and emotionally rich.

ONE OF THE KEY CHALLENGES with dynamics is knowing **when to use them**. Too many dynamic shifts can make a song feel chaotic or disjointed, while too few can make it feel monotonous. The key is to think about the emotional arc of your song and how dynamics can help tell that story. If your song is about building towards an emotional peak, a crescendo might be the perfect way to mirror that feeling. If it's about sudden heartbreak, an abrupt dynamic shift could convey the shock and intensity of that moment.

When thinking about dynamics, also consider the **space** between the notes. Silence or near-silence can be just as powerful as a loud section. Dropping down to almost no sound before building back up can create a sense of anticipation and make the next loud section hit even harder. *In the Air Tonight* by Phil Collins famously uses this technique, with the long, sparse buildup before the iconic drum fill that catapults the song into its final, dramatic section.

Incorporating dynamics into your songwriting involves not just crafting a melody and harmony but thinking about **how** that music is delivered—how it breathes, moves, and interacts with the listener on an emotional level. Whether you're building toward a soaring crescendo, using silence to create tension, or layering instruments for a dynamic build, the way you play with volume and intensity is a powerful storytelling tool. Dynamics give you control over the energy of your song, allowing you to guide the listener through peaks and valleys of emotion.

In the end, dynamics are about contrast and storytelling. By carefully choosing when to go loud, when to stay quiet, and how to navigate the spaces in between, you can create songs that captivate listeners, evoke deep emotions, and leave a lasting impact.

Tonality: Setting the Mood with Key Choices

Tonality, or the choice of key, is one of the most important decisions you'll make when writing a song. It can subtly influence the emotional impact of your music and set the mood even before the lyrics or melody come into play. While the key you choose might seem like a technical aspect of songwriting, it's deeply tied to the emotional tone of your song and plays a vital role in how the listener experiences your music. By understanding how different keys and tonalities can shape the feel of a song, you can harness tonality as a powerful tool for expression.

In music, tonality refers to the organization of pitches around a central note, called the **tonic**. The tonic is the "home" note that provides stability and resolution throughout the song. For example, in the key of C major, the note C is the tonic, and the other notes in the key—D, E, F, G, A, and B—revolve around it. When a song is in a major key, it tends to evoke a brighter, more uplifting mood, while a song in a minor key often feels darker, sadder, or more introspective.

One of the most fundamental choices you'll make in tonality is whether to write your song in a **major or minor key**. Major keys, with their intervals structured to create a sense of brightness and openness, are often associated with emotions like happiness, confidence, and hope. On the other hand, minor keys, which have a flattened third note compared to major keys, give a sense of melancholy, tension, or mystery. This difference between major and minor is one of the reasons certain songs can feel upbeat and joyful, while others convey a sense of longing or sadness.

Take, for instance, Bob Dylan's *Blowin' in the Wind*, which is written in a major key. The major tonality gives the song a feeling of optimism and resilience, despite its serious subject matter. Contrast that with a song like *Hurt* by Nine Inch Nails (famously covered by Johnny Cash), which is in a minor key. The minor tonality of *Hurt* amplifies the song's emotional weight, conveying a deep sense of pain and introspection.

Tonality doesn't just affect the overall mood—it also impacts the **color** and **texture** of a song. Each key has its own unique "color," which can affect how a listener perceives the song. For example, the key of C major is often described as bright and clear, while the key of D minor is thought of as somber or even dramatic. These associations aren't strict rules, but many musicians feel a difference in how certain keys resonate emotionally. Beethoven, for instance, famously referred to B minor as the "black key," associating it with feelings of despair and tragedy.

Beyond the basic choice of major or minor, you can explore different **modes** to expand your tonal palette. Modes are alternative scales that can be derived from the standard major scale but produce different emotional effects. For example, the **Dorian mode** (which is similar to the natural minor scale but with a raised sixth note) can create a feeling of wistful sadness mixed with a touch of hope, as heard in many folk and jazz tunes. Meanwhile, the **Mixolydian mode** (which is like the major scale but with a flattened seventh) is often used in rock and blues to give a song a slightly edgy, rebellious feel.

One of the fascinating things about tonality is how it interacts with a song's **lyrics and story**. Sometimes, the key can amplify the emotional content of the lyrics, as when a sad lyric is paired with a minor key. Other times, a songwriter might choose to contrast the tonality with the lyrics to create an interesting emotional dynamic. For instance, pairing upbeat, happy lyrics with a major key can feel like a natural fit, but writing joyful lyrics in a minor key can give the song a bittersweet or ironic twist. The Smiths often used this technique, crafting upbeat, jangly melodies in major keys while their lyrics explored darker, more melancholic themes, creating a sense of contrast that resonated deeply with listeners.

Another powerful tool in tonality is **modulation**, or changing keys within a song. Modulating to a new key can introduce a sense of excitement, tension, or resolution. Many pop and rock songs use key changes (often up a whole step) to add intensity, especially in the final chorus, making the song feel like it's reaching a climactic point. One famous example is Whitney Houston's *I Will Always Love You*, where the key change in the final chorus elevates the emotional intensity of the song, giving it a powerful, dramatic finish. Modulating to a new key can make a song feel like it's evolving, heightening the listener's emotional engagement.

You can also explore **modal interchange**, where you borrow chords from a parallel key (for example, borrowing minor chords from the parallel minor key while in a major key). This technique can add emotional complexity and unpredictability to your song. The Beatles were masters of this, often using modal interchange to add unexpected harmonic twists that gave their songs a unique emotional depth. A song like *Something* by George Harrison (performed by The Beatles) moves between major and minor chords in a way that creates a rich, layered emotional experience.

Tonality also interacts with **instrumentation**. A song in a major key played on a bright, jangly guitar might feel cheerful and open, while the same key played on a piano or a string section might evoke a different, more nuanced emotional tone. Consider the way Radiohead's *No Surprises* uses the key of F major, typically a "happy" key, but pairs it with delicate, melancholy instrumentation and understated vocals to create a song that feels reflective and somber, despite its major tonality. The combination of tonality and the texture of the instrumentation gives the song its unique emotional flavor.

When choosing the key for your song, don't just think about the technical aspects—consider how the key feels and how it fits with the mood you want to convey. Play your song in different keys and notice how the shift in tonality changes the emotional impact. Sometimes, a slight shift in key can make the song feel more comfortable for the singer's range or give the chords a richer, fuller sound. For example, moving from C major to A major might make the song feel brighter, while shifting from A minor to G minor could make it feel darker or more introspective.

BEYOND MAJOR AND MINOR, **chromaticism** (using notes outside of the key) can add unexpected tension and interest. By briefly moving outside the established tonality of your song, you can create moments of surprise that heighten the emotional impact when you return to the home key. Chromatic passing tones or chords can give a song a more sophisticated, nuanced sound, as seen in jazz or classical music, but they can also be used effectively in pop and rock. David Bowie often used chromaticism to create a sense of unease or otherworldliness in his music, adding to his songs' emotional and psychological complexity.

Finally, tonality is about **creating a world** for your song. The key you choose is the foundation of that world, influencing everything from the harmonic structure to the emotional arc of the music. By carefully selecting your key and experimenting with different tonal options, you can craft a musical landscape that aligns perfectly with the mood, message, and meaning of your song.

In the end, tonality is more than just a technical choice—it's a deeply emotional one. The key you choose shapes the listener's experience, guiding their emotional response to your music. Whether you're working in a major key to convey brightness and hope, or exploring the depths of a minor key to evoke introspection and longing, tonality is the heart of your song's emotional core. By experimenting with different keys, modes, and harmonic techniques, you can unlock new layers of expression and craft songs that resonate powerfully with your audience.

Instrumentation: Choosing the Right Sounds for Your Song

Instrumentation is one of the most vital components of songwriting, as it determines the overall sound and texture of your music. The instruments you choose, how they are arranged, and the way they interact with one another all contribute to the emotional and sonic landscape of your song. A well-chosen combination of instruments can elevate a simple melody, enhance the mood, and make your song more engaging and memorable. The right instrumentation not only supports the song but also defines its character, giving it a unique identity that resonates with listeners.

When choosing instrumentation, the first thing to consider is the **genre** and **style** of your song. Different genres have their own traditional sets of instruments that help establish the musical world of the song. For example, rock songs often rely on electric guitar, bass, and drums as the core instrumentation, while folk music might feature acoustic guitars, banjos, or mandolins. Understanding the conventions of your genre can guide your initial choices, but it's important to remember that genre boundaries are fluid. Many successful songs creatively mix instruments from different genres to create fresh, unexpected sounds.

Take for instance *Seven Nation Army* by The White Stripes. The song is primarily driven by a bassline that sounds like it's played on a bass guitar, but it's actually Jack White's electric guitar run through a pitch-shifting pedal. This unconventional choice in instrumentation gives the song a distinctive sound that helped it stand out and become iconic. By stepping outside the typical instrumentation for rock music, The White Stripes created something new and memorable. This example shows that while traditional instrumentation works well, experimentation can give your song a unique edge.

Beyond genre conventions, consider the **emotional tone** of your song. Each instrument has its own sonic qualities, and different instruments can evoke different feelings. A piano might bring a sense of elegance or melancholy, while a distorted electric guitar can add aggression or energy. Strings, such as violins or cellos, can introduce warmth or drama, while synthesizers can create a futuristic or ethereal atmosphere. When writing your song, think about the emotions you want to convey and choose instruments that match that mood. For example, if you're writing a ballad about heartbreak, a soft piano or acoustic guitar might provide the intimacy needed to support the vulnerability of the lyrics. On the other hand, if you're writing an anthemic song about overcoming obstacles, adding a soaring lead guitar or powerful drums could enhance the sense of triumph.

Contrast and balance are key considerations when selecting instruments. Too many instruments in the same frequency range can make your song sound cluttered, while too few can leave it feeling sparse. Striking the right balance means thinking about how the instruments work together sonically. For example, pairing a bass guitar with a higher-pitched instrument like a mandolin or violin creates a pleasing contrast, allowing each instrument to shine without competing for the same sonic space. This balance can be achieved by assigning different roles to each instrument, such as using the bass to anchor the low end, the guitar to fill the midrange, and a keyboard or synth to add brightness and texture to the high end.

Sometimes, less is more. **Minimal instrumentation** can be just as effective, if not more so, than a full band arrangement. Stripping a song down to just one or two instruments can create an intimate, raw atmosphere. This is particularly effective in acoustic or singer-songwriter genres, where the focus is often on the lyrics and melody. By keeping the instrumentation minimal, you allow the song's emotional core to shine through without distractions. Johnny Cash's cover of *Hurt* is a perfect example of this approach. The sparse arrangement, featuring only acoustic guitar and piano, highlights the vulnerability and raw emotion of the song, allowing Cash's vocals to take center stage.

On the other hand, **layering multiple instruments** can add depth and richness to a song. Layering involves adding different instruments, each playing complementary parts, to create a full, immersive sound. For example, you might layer acoustic and electric guitars to add both warmth and punch, or blend strings with synths to create a lush, cinematic atmosphere. When layering instruments, pay attention to how they interact in terms of timing, texture, and tone. Too many layers can muddy the sound, but when done right, layering can create a dynamic and engaging soundscape that evolves throughout the song.

One way to explore instrumentation is to think about the **role** of each instrument within the song. The **rhythm section**, which typically includes drums, bass, and rhythm guitar or keyboard, provides the foundation of the song. The rhythm section's job is to establish the groove and keep the song grounded, driving the music forward while leaving room for the melody and harmony to shine. When choosing instruments for the rhythm section, think about how they'll work together to create a cohesive pulse. For example, a tight, syncopated bassline can complement a steady drum beat, while an acoustic guitar might provide a rhythmic strumming pattern that fills out the midrange.

The **lead instruments**, such as lead guitar, piano, or vocals, are responsible for delivering the melody and taking the spotlight. These instruments often have more room to explore dynamics, phrasing, and expressive techniques. When choosing lead instruments, consider how they complement each other and the overall vibe of the song. For instance, a guitar solo might add an energetic break in a rock song, while a piano melody could add elegance or melancholy in a ballad. It's important to balance the prominence of the lead instruments with the supporting instruments so that the lead parts stand out without overwhelming the rest of the arrangement.

Don't underestimate the power of **unusual or unexpected instruments** to add character to your song. Incorporating non-traditional instruments or sounds can give your music a distinctive edge. For example, using a banjo in a pop song or a synthesizer in a folk tune can introduce a fresh, surprising element that grabs the listener's attention. The Beatles often experimented with unconventional instruments, such as the sitar in *Norwegian Wood* or the string octet in *Eleanor Rigby*, to add new dimensions to their sound. These unique choices helped define the band's creative evolution and made their music stand out.

———————

ANOTHER LAYER OF DEPTH can be added through **sound effects and non-instrumental elements**. Sometimes, the right atmosphere for your song isn't achieved solely through traditional instruments. Sound effects like ambient noise, nature sounds, or industrial textures can be incorporated to enhance the emotional and thematic content of a song. For example, in Pink Floyd's *Money*, the use of cash register sounds and coin clinking reinforces the lyrical theme of materialism and greed. These non-musical elements are part of the instrumentation that helps create a full, immersive experience for the listener.

Instrumentation also plays a significant role in defining the **dynamics** of a song. By introducing or removing instruments throughout different sections, you can create contrast, build tension, or provide resolution. For instance, starting a song with a simple piano line and gradually introducing drums, bass, and guitar as the song progresses can create a sense of build-up and anticipation. Conversely, stripping the instrumentation back during a bridge or final verse can make a song feel more intimate and reflective. The way you introduce or withdraw instruments over the course of a song can shape its emotional arc and make certain moments feel more impactful.

Finally, think about how your chosen instruments will affect the **live performance** of your song. If you plan to perform the song live, it's important to consider how the instrumentation will translate to the stage. Some songs might be easy to replicate live with just a guitar and a vocalist, while others might require a full band or even orchestral backing. Simplifying the instrumentation for live performances can be effective, especially if the song's core elements—melody, rhythm, and emotion—are strong enough to stand on their own.

In the end, choosing the right instrumentation for your song is about balancing the technical and emotional aspects of music. The instruments you select should serve the song's purpose, enhancing its mood, message, and overall feel. Whether you opt for a minimalist acoustic arrangement or a lush, layered production, the goal is to create a sonic world that supports and amplifies the core of your song. By carefully considering how each instrument contributes to that world, you can craft a sound that resonates with your audience and makes your music memorable.

Common Chord Progressions in Songwriting

Chord progressions are the backbone of most songs, providing the harmonic foundation that supports the melody and lyrics. While there are countless ways to arrange chords, certain progressions have stood the test of time, becoming staples in popular music due to their emotional resonance and accessibility. These progressions create a sense of familiarity and structure that listeners can connect with, while also offering a solid starting point for songwriters to build upon. Understanding and mastering these common chord progressions is a key step in developing your songwriting skills.

At its core, a chord progression is simply a series of chords played in a specific sequence. Each chord creates a certain feeling, and the way these chords move from one to the next can evoke different emotional responses. Some progressions create tension, while others offer resolution or a sense of uplift. The magic of chord progressions lies in how they combine harmony and movement to support the overall mood of the song.

One of the most widely used and recognizable chord progressions in Western music is the **I-IV-V progression**. This progression is built on the first (I), fourth (IV), and fifth (V) chords of a major scale. In the key of C major, for example, the chords would be C (I), F (IV), and G (V). This progression forms the harmonic backbone of countless songs across genres, from rock and pop to blues and country. Its appeal lies in its simplicity and versatility—it creates a sense of tension and resolution, with the V chord (G) leading back to the I chord (C) for a satisfying conclusion. Songs like *Twist and Shout* by The Beatles and *Wild Thing* by The Troggs are built around this classic progression.

The I-IV-V progression works so well because it creates a natural **harmonic movement**. The IV chord (F) feels like a step away from home, while the V chord (G) introduces tension, making the return to the I chord (C) feel like a resolution. This basic pattern is easy to play, easy to remember, and creates a feeling of stability and familiarity, which is why it's used so frequently in popular music. Even though it's simple, there's plenty of room for variation. You can try changing the rhythm, adding chord inversions, or experimenting with melody to make this progression your own.

Another incredibly popular progression is the **I-V-vi-IV progression**, sometimes referred to as the "Axis of Awesome" progression due to its use in many modern pop songs. In the key of C, this progression would be C (I), G (V), A minor (vi), and F (IV). This progression has a slightly more emotional, reflective quality than the I-IV-V progression because of the presence of the minor vi chord, which introduces a touch of sadness or longing. Despite this, it still maintains a sense of movement and resolution, making it a go-to choice for many songwriters. Songs like *Let It Be* by The Beatles, *With or Without You* by U2, and *Someone Like You* by Adele all use this progression, demonstrating its versatility and emotional depth.

THE I-V-VI-IV PROGRESSION is popular because it strikes a balance between **major and minor chords**, creating an emotional complexity that resonates with listeners. The shift between major and minor chords evokes a bittersweet feeling—uplifting but with a hint of melancholy. This progression works particularly well in ballads, love songs, and anthemic pop tracks, where the interplay between hope and longing is often central to the song's emotional message.

A third essential chord progression is the **ii-V-I progression**, which is a staple in jazz but has found its way into many other genres as well. In this progression, the ii chord (the minor second chord in the scale) leads to the V chord, which then resolves to the I chord. In the key of C, this would be D minor (ii), G (V), and C (I). The ii-V-I progression creates a smooth, logical flow of harmony that feels elegant and complete. It's a bit more sophisticated than the I-IV-V progression and is often used in more harmonically rich songs, as it allows for interesting melodic possibilities and complex jazz chords, such as sevenths and ninths.

The ii-V-I progression is perfect for creating a sense of movement, especially in jazz or more complex pop compositions. Because it passes through a minor chord (ii) on the way to the V chord, it adds a layer of **tension** that is beautifully resolved when the progression returns to the I chord. Many jazz standards, like *Autumn Leaves* and *All the Things You Are*, use this progression extensively, making it an important tool for songwriters who want to explore more advanced harmonic territory.

Another chord progression that has been used across decades and genres is the **I-vi-IV-V progression**, often called the "1950s progression" or "doo-wop progression" due to its frequent use in 1950s pop songs. In the key of C, this progression would be C (I), A minor (vi), F (IV), and G (V). This progression has a nostalgic, feel-good vibe, and it's still used today because of its catchiness and emotional warmth. Songs like *Stand by Me* by Ben E. King, *Earth Angel* by The Penguins, and *Every Breath You Take* by The Police all use variations of this progression.

The **vi-IV-I-V progression** is a closely related variation that's equally popular, particularly in modern pop music. This rearrangement of the chords (in the key of C: A minor, F, C, G) shifts the focus to the minor vi chord, giving the progression a slightly darker, more emotional edge. This progression has been used in songs like *Apologize* by OneRepublic and *She Will Be Loved* by Maroon 5, demonstrating its appeal for more emotionally charged, introspective music.

For songwriters looking to add **tension and drama**, the **IV-I-V progression**, also known as the "plagal cadence" or "amen cadence," can be a powerful tool. In this progression, the IV chord resolves directly to the I chord without passing through the dominant (V) chord. In the key of C, this would be F (IV) to C (I). This progression is often used at the end of hymns and religious music because of its strong, conclusive feel, but it can also be used creatively in popular music to add a different kind of resolution. The Beatles used this progression in *Let It Be*, giving the song a peaceful, almost spiritual quality.

FOR MORE **emotional complexity**, you might want to explore the **I-vi-ii-V progression**, which in the key of C would be C (I), A minor (vi), D minor (ii), and G (V). This progression, sometimes called the "circle progression," moves through both major and minor chords in a way that feels natural and satisfying, with a clear sense of forward motion. It's common in jazz, doo-wop, and pop ballads, and its combination of major and minor chords offers a wide range of emotional expression.

Understanding these common chord progressions provides you with a toolkit for songwriting. Once you're familiar with these progressions, you can begin to **experiment** with variations, substitutions, and inversions to create something uniquely your own. For example, you could add a **secondary dominant** chord (a dominant seventh chord that leads to a chord other than the tonic) to spice up a simple progression. In the key of C, a secondary dominant might be D7 leading into G, creating a more dynamic transition from the ii to the V chord.

You can also explore **modulation**—changing keys within the song—to create contrast or shift the emotional tone. Many pop and rock songs use a key change (often up a whole step) in the final chorus to elevate the energy and emotional impact of the song.

Ultimately, chord progressions are about **emotion** and **movement**. They guide the listener through the song, providing structure and direction while enhancing the mood of the melody and lyrics. Whether you're writing a simple three-chord song or experimenting with more complex progressions, understanding the basics of harmony allows you to make intentional choices that serve the song and resonate with your audience. By mastering these common progressions and learning how to manipulate them creatively, you'll have the foundation you need to craft songs that are both familiar and original.

Telling a Story through Lyrics

Telling a story through lyrics is one of the most powerful ways to connect with listeners. A well-told story not only captures attention but also evokes emotions, draws listeners into a world of experience, and leaves a lasting impression. While melody, rhythm, and harmony all contribute to the emotional impact of a song, it's often the lyrics that give the song its narrative depth and meaning. Crafting lyrics that tell a compelling story requires a combination of creativity, structure, and emotional honesty.

At the heart of storytelling in songwriting is the **narrative arc**. Just like in a novel or film, a song's lyrics should have a beginning, middle, and end. Even if the song is short, this arc helps guide the listener through a journey. The song might tell a literal story with characters, setting, and a plot, or it might explore an emotional journey that mirrors the same structure, moving from conflict or tension to resolution.

One of the most important aspects of storytelling in lyrics is **choosing a focal point**. A good story doesn't try to cover everything—it zooms in on a particular moment, experience, or emotion. When writing lyrics, ask yourself: What's the main theme or story I want to tell? It could be about falling in love, going through heartbreak, overcoming adversity, or reflecting on a meaningful event. Focusing on a specific moment or theme gives your lyrics clarity and purpose, allowing listeners to engage with the story on a personal level.

For example, in Bruce Springsteen's *The River*, the lyrics tell the story of a young couple facing the challenges of life in a small town. Springsteen uses specific details—working in construction, getting married young, and facing economic hardship—to paint a vivid picture of their struggles. By focusing on these concrete experiences, the song tells a personal and relatable story while exploring broader themes of love, loss, and hope. This balance between specific details and universal themes is one of the keys to effective storytelling in songwriting.

Setting the scene is another crucial element in lyrical storytelling. Just like in a novel or short story, the setting of a song helps ground the listener in a specific time and place. Whether you're writing about a real location or an imagined one, providing a sense of atmosphere helps the listener visualize the story. You don't need to describe every detail, but using sensory imagery—sights, sounds, smells, or textures—can transport the listener into the world of the song.

Consider Bob Dylan's *Tangled Up in Blue*, where the lyrics weave together fragmented scenes of different times and places. Dylan's use of vivid, specific imagery—like "a topless place" or "the banks of the river"—creates a sense of movement and atmosphere, allowing the listener to follow the narrative as it jumps through time. This ability to paint pictures with words is essential for effective storytelling in song lyrics.

CHARACTERS are another vital part of lyrical storytelling. While not every song needs defined characters, many memorable songs introduce people who serve as focal points for the narrative. These characters could be real or fictional, and they often serve as vehicles for the songwriter to explore emotions, conflicts, and relationships. Introducing a character in your song gives listeners someone to connect with, helping to humanize the narrative.

For example, in Dolly Parton's *Jolene*, the titular character becomes the embodiment of jealousy and fear. Parton addresses Jolene directly in the lyrics, creating an intimate dialogue between the narrator and this mysterious, almost mythical woman. The simplicity of the storytelling, combined with the raw emotion expressed in the lyrics, makes *Jolene* an unforgettable tale of love and vulnerability. The character of Jolene gives the song its emotional center, allowing the listener to feel the narrator's desperation and fear of loss.

Conflict is a key element in any good story, and songwriting is no exception. Whether it's an external conflict between characters or an internal struggle, conflict creates tension and keeps the listener engaged. Without conflict, a song can feel static or uninteresting. In lyrical storytelling, conflict often comes in the form of emotional challenges—heartbreak, loss, betrayal, or longing.

In Fleetwood Mac's *Go Your Own Way*, the conflict is clear from the start: a broken relationship. The lyrics capture the pain and frustration of a love that's falling apart, with lines like "Loving you isn't the right thing to do" expressing the internal turmoil of the narrator. The tension between wanting to hold on and needing to let go drives the emotional narrative, making the song both relatable and powerful.

Once you've established the conflict, the lyrics should move toward some form of **resolution**. This doesn't necessarily mean a happy ending—many great songs end on a note of ambiguity or unresolved emotion—but the story should feel complete. A song's resolution might involve the narrator coming to terms with a difficult truth, finding hope in the face of adversity, or accepting loss. The resolution gives the song a sense of closure, even if it's an open-ended one.

A great example of this is *Fast Car* by Tracy Chapman. The song tells the story of a woman trying to escape a life of poverty and hardship. The conflict is established early on as she dreams of a better life with her partner, but as the song progresses, it becomes clear that those dreams are slipping away. The final verse brings a somber resolution, as the narrator realizes that nothing has changed and she's still stuck in the same place. The song's ending is bittersweet, with the resolution reflecting the harsh reality of the narrator's situation.

In addition to narrative structure, **emotion** is the driving force behind any great story in songwriting. Lyrics are often most powerful when they convey raw, authentic emotions. Whether you're writing about joy, heartbreak, anger, or hope, it's important to tap into genuine feelings that resonate with both you and your audience. Listeners connect with songs that reflect their own experiences, and emotion is the bridge that allows them to relate to your story.

One of the best ways to convey emotion in your lyrics is through **specificity**. Rather than using vague or generic phrases, focus on concrete details that bring the emotion to life. For example, instead of saying "I'm sad," describe what sadness feels like: "The room is cold, and the light feels gray," or "I can't remember the last time I laughed." These details make the emotion more tangible and relatable, allowing the listener to step inside the story.

In John Prine's *Sam Stone*, the lyrics tell the story of a Vietnam War veteran who struggles with addiction after returning home. Prine's use of specific details—like "Sam Stone came home to his wife and family / After serving in the conflict overseas"—grounds the song in a real, visceral experience, making the emotional weight of the story all the more impactful. The specificity of the lyrics allows listeners to empathize with Sam's tragic journey, even if they've never experienced anything like it themselves.

Point of view is another important consideration when telling a story through lyrics. The perspective you choose can shape how the story is received and interpreted. First-person lyrics create an intimate connection between the narrator and the listener, as the story is told from a personal, subjective point of view. This can be particularly effective for emotional or introspective songs. Third-person lyrics, on the other hand, provide more distance, allowing you to tell the story from an outsider's perspective. Both approaches have their advantages, and the choice of point of view should depend on the kind of story you want to tell.

In addition to narrative structure and emotion, **repetition** can be a powerful tool in storytelling. Repeating certain phrases or lines can reinforce the central theme of the song, helping to drive home the emotional impact. Many folk and blues songs use repetition to create a sense of rhythm and continuity in the story. For example, in Bob Dylan's *The Times They Are A-Changin'*, the repeated line "The times they are a-changin'" serves as both a chorus and a thematic anchor for the entire song, emphasizing the inevitability of social change.

Ultimately, telling a story through lyrics is about **connecting with the listener**. Whether you're telling a personal tale, exploring universal themes, or creating fictional characters, the goal is to evoke emotions and create a narrative that resonates. By combining structure, specificity, emotion, and a clear point of view, you can craft lyrics that draw listeners in and leave a lasting impact. Storytelling through song is one of the oldest and most powerful forms of human expression, and when done well, it can make your music not just heard but felt.

Lessons from Neil Young: Raw Emotion in Songwriting

Neil Young is a master of emotional authenticity in songwriting. Across his long and prolific career, he has demonstrated an unparalleled ability to tap into raw, unfiltered emotion, connecting deeply with listeners through songs that are both personal and universal. From his deeply introspective ballads to his politically charged anthems, Young's work offers valuable lessons for songwriters seeking to inject their own music with emotional depth and sincerity.

One of the key lessons from Neil Young's songwriting is the power of **emotional honesty**. Young's songs are often intensely personal, dealing with themes like love, loss, isolation, and longing, but they are never melodramatic or forced. Instead, his lyrics are straightforward, unembellished, and often written in plain language. This emotional honesty allows listeners to connect with his songs on a deep level because they feel real—there's no pretense, no attempt to impress. Young is known for writing about the things that matter most to him, even when those things are difficult or uncomfortable to express.

In songs like *Heart of Gold*, Young captures the feeling of yearning and searching for something deeper in life. The lyrics are simple but profound: "I want to live, I want to give / I've been a miner for a heart of gold." These lines convey a universal sense of longing for meaning and connection, and they do so in a way that feels personal, as though Young is speaking directly to the listener. The emotional power of the song lies in its honesty and vulnerability. Young isn't afraid to reveal his own sense of incompleteness, and that vulnerability invites listeners to reflect on their own experiences.

Young's use of **simplicity** in lyrics and music is another important lesson for songwriters. While many artists strive for complex wordplay or intricate compositions, Young often pares things down to their most basic elements. His songs are rarely overproduced, and the lyrics are often sparse, leaving room for the listener to fill in the emotional blanks. This simplicity allows the emotions to shine through more clearly. In songs like *Old Man* or *The Needle and the Damage Done*, Young uses straightforward language to express deep, complex emotions, giving the songs a raw, direct impact.

In *The Needle and the Damage Done*, Young addresses the devastating effects of heroin addiction in just a few short verses. The song is stark and haunting, with minimal instrumentation and a simple melody. The lyrics, "I've seen the needle and the damage done / A little part of it in everyone," convey the sorrow and helplessness of witnessing a friend's struggle with addiction. The simplicity of the lyrics and music mirrors the starkness of the subject matter, making the song feel raw and real. By avoiding elaborate metaphors or complicated arrangements, Young allows the emotional core of the song to take center stage.

Another hallmark of Neil Young's songwriting is his willingness to embrace **imperfection**. In an industry where polished production and flawless performances are often the goal, Young has consistently chosen authenticity over perfection. His voice, which is high-pitched and slightly nasal, doesn't fit the traditional mold of a "perfect" singing voice, but it's part of what makes his music so emotionally resonant. Young's vocal delivery is filled with cracks and quivers, and it's this vulnerability that gives his songs their emotional weight.

Young's live performances are similarly unpolished, often featuring moments of spontaneity or imperfection that add to the raw emotional energy of the music. In his song *Cowgirl in the Sand*, the extended guitar solos feel loose and exploratory, as though Young is following his emotions rather than sticking to a prearranged plan. This willingness to embrace imperfection in both his songwriting and performance creates an intimate connection with the listener, as though Young is inviting them into his world, flaws and all.

A key lesson from Neil Young is the importance of **personal truth** in songwriting. Young has never shied away from writing about what he believes in, whether it's personal struggles or political views. His willingness to take a stand and write about difficult, controversial topics has set him apart as an artist who writes from the heart, without concern for commercial success or mainstream approval. Songs like *Ohio*, which was written in response to the Kent State shootings, show Young's commitment to using his music as a platform for addressing real-world issues. The lyrics of *Ohio* are blunt and direct: "Tin soldiers and Nixon's comin' / We're finally on our own / This summer I hear the drummin' / Four dead in Ohio." There's no attempt to soften the message or make it more palatable—the raw emotion and anger are front and center.

Young's ability to fuse the **personal and the political** is another valuable lesson for songwriters. While many of his songs are deeply personal, they often resonate on a broader, universal level. In *Ohio*, Young taps into the collective outrage and grief of a nation, while in *After the Gold Rush*, he uses personal reflection to comment on environmental destruction and human folly. The song's dreamlike lyrics, "Look at Mother Nature on the run / In the nineteen seventies," are both a personal lament and a broader social commentary, showing how songwriting can be both introspective and outward-looking at the same time.

In addition to his lyrical prowess, Young's use of **instrumentation and arrangement** also contributes to the raw emotional power of his songs. Whether he's playing acoustic guitar, electric guitar with Crazy Horse, or the piano, Young's arrangements are often sparse and unadorned, allowing the emotion of the song to come through clearly. In songs like *Helpless*, the stripped-down instrumentation creates a sense of vulnerability and openness that mirrors the lyrics. The repetitive, droning chord progression adds to the feeling of helplessness and melancholy, reinforcing the song's emotional message.

Even when Young does use more complex arrangements, as in *Like a Hurricane*, the intensity of the music mirrors the emotional intensity of the lyrics. The extended guitar solos in *Like a Hurricane* feel like a storm of emotion, with the wailing guitar lines expressing the turbulence of the narrator's feelings. Young's use of electric guitar is often visceral and raw, adding a layer of emotional depth to his songs that goes beyond the lyrics.

ANOTHER IMPORTANT LESSON from Neil Young's songwriting is the use of **repetition and thematic development**. Many of Young's songs revolve around simple, repeated phrases or musical motifs that build in emotional intensity as the song progresses. In *Cortez the Killer*, for example, the repeated chord progression and recurring imagery of the conqueror Cortez create a hypnotic, meditative effect, drawing the listener deeper into the narrative and the emotions behind it. The repetition of the musical and lyrical themes allows the listener to focus on the emotional undercurrents of the song, making it more immersive and impactful.

Ultimately, one of the greatest lessons Neil Young offers songwriters is the importance of **authenticity**. Young has always followed his own path, writing music that reflects his personal experiences, beliefs, and emotions, rather than conforming to industry trends or expectations. His commitment to writing from a place of honesty and vulnerability has earned him a devoted following and made his songs timeless.

For songwriters, the takeaway is clear: to write songs that resonate, you must be willing to be open, honest, and true to yourself. By embracing imperfection, telling personal truths, and expressing raw emotion, you can create music that connects with listeners on a deep, emotional level. Neil Young's music reminds us that it's not about perfection—it's about conveying real emotions, even when they're messy, complex, or uncomfortable. That's where the magic of songwriting lies.

Lessons from Bob Dylan: The Art of Storytelling through Songs

Bob Dylan is widely regarded as one of the greatest songwriters of all time, and his ability to tell stories through his songs has had a profound influence on generations of musicians. Whether crafting protest songs, love ballads, or surreal narratives, Dylan's work showcases the power of storytelling in music. His lyrics are often layered with symbolism, historical references, and personal insights, creating songs that feel as relevant today as when they were first written. For songwriters, there is much to learn from Dylan's approach to storytelling, from his use of vivid imagery and character development to his unconventional song structures.

One of the first lessons from Bob Dylan is the importance of **vivid imagery** in storytelling. Dylan's lyrics are rich with visual details that draw listeners into the world of the song. He often paints pictures with his words, allowing the audience to see, hear, and feel the scenes he describes. In *Tangled Up in Blue*, for example, Dylan takes the listener on a journey through fragmented memories of a relationship, using images like "a topless place" and "a basement down the stairs" to evoke a sense of time and place. These specific, often unusual details make the story come alive, engaging the listener's imagination.

When telling a story through lyrics, it's not enough to simply recount events. Great storytelling involves **showing rather than telling**, and Dylan excels at this. Instead of stating emotions directly, he uses imagery to convey them. In *Like a Rolling Stone*, he doesn't just tell the listener that the protagonist has fallen from grace; instead, he uses lines like, "You used to be so amused / At Napoleon in rags and the language that he used / Go to him now, he calls you, you can't refuse," to illustrate the character's loss of status and control. By letting the details speak for themselves, Dylan invites the listener to interpret the story and feel its emotional impact more deeply.

Dylan also shows that **character development** is crucial to effective storytelling. Many of his songs are populated by vivid, complex characters who serve as the focal points of the narrative. These characters are often deeply flawed, reflective of real human struggles and contradictions. In *Hurricane*, Dylan tells the true story of Rubin "Hurricane" Carter, a boxer wrongfully convicted of murder. Dylan's portrayal of Carter is both empathetic and compelling, painting him as a victim of racial injustice, while also highlighting the systemic corruption that framed him. The character of Hurricane comes alive in the song, and through him, Dylan comments on larger social issues.

Dylan's ability to weave **political and social commentary** into his storytelling is another important lesson for songwriters. Songs like *The Times They Are A-Changin'* and *Blowin' in the Wind* are protest songs that speak to the social upheavals of their time, but they are also universal enough to resonate decades later. Dylan often writes about historical or political events in a way that feels personal and immediate, grounding abstract issues in the lives and experiences of ordinary people. In *The Lonesome Death of Hattie Carroll*, for example, Dylan recounts the true story of a Black woman killed by a wealthy white man, exposing the racial injustices of the time. The song doesn't preach; instead, it tells the story in a way that allows the listener to draw their own conclusions.

Another hallmark of Dylan's storytelling is his use of **narrative perspective**. He often shifts between different points of view, which adds complexity and depth to his stories. In some songs, Dylan adopts the voice of a narrator who observes events from the outside, while in others, he takes on the perspective of the character within the story. In *Ballad of a Thin Man*, Dylan addresses the protagonist, Mr. Jones, directly, creating an accusatory and confrontational tone. This shifting perspective keeps the listener engaged, as they are drawn into the narrative from different angles.

Dylan's approach to **song structure** is another valuable lesson for songwriters. He frequently breaks away from traditional verse-chorus-verse structures, opting for longer, more free-flowing forms that allow the story to unfold naturally. In songs like *A Hard Rain's A-Gonna Fall* and *Desolation Row*, Dylan uses long verses that build on one another, gradually revealing the layers of the story. These songs don't rely on a catchy chorus or hook to keep the listener engaged—instead, it's the strength of the narrative and the unfolding imagery that captures attention.

Dylan's willingness to **embrace complexity** in his storytelling is one of the reasons his songs resonate so deeply. He doesn't shy away from ambiguity or contradiction, and his lyrics often leave room for multiple interpretations. In *Visions of Johanna*, for instance, Dylan weaves together surreal images and fragmented scenes that never quite coalesce into a clear narrative, yet the song still conveys a powerful sense of longing and disillusionment. This openness allows listeners to bring their own experiences and emotions to the song, making the story feel more personal and universal at the same time.

Symbolism and metaphor play a central role in Dylan's songwriting. Rather than presenting stories in a straightforward way, he often uses symbols and metaphors to suggest deeper meanings. In *Mr. Tambourine Man*, for example, the tambourine man becomes a symbol of escape, freedom, and creativity, while the song itself explores themes of disillusionment and the search for meaning. Dylan's use of metaphor allows him to tell stories that operate on multiple levels, combining literal narrative with symbolic exploration of bigger themes.

Another lesson from Dylan's storytelling is his ability to convey **social and personal change**. His songs often explore themes of transformation, whether it's personal growth, societal upheaval, or the passing of time. In *The Times They Are A-Changin'*, Dylan captures the spirit of social revolution, urging people to embrace change and adapt to the new world that's coming. This sense of transformation is also present in songs like *Tangled Up in Blue*, where the protagonist reflects on the changes that have occurred in his life and relationships. Dylan's ability to tell stories of change resonates with listeners because it reflects the universal human experience of growth, loss, and adaptation.

Dylan's use of **repetition and refrain** is another effective storytelling technique. In many of his songs, repeated phrases or lines serve as thematic anchors, tying the narrative together and reinforcing key ideas. For instance, in *Blowin' in the Wind*, the repeated refrain, "The answer, my friend, is blowin' in the wind," serves as both a metaphorical and literal question, leaving the listener to ponder the meaning. Repetition creates a sense of rhythm and structure in Dylan's songs, while also emphasizing the central themes of the story.

Finally, Dylan's **fearlessness in tackling difficult subjects** is one of the most valuable lessons for songwriters. He isn't afraid to write about controversial or uncomfortable topics, whether it's war, racism, injustice, or existential despair. This willingness to confront difficult issues head-on gives his songs a sense of urgency and relevance, even decades after they were written. In *Masters of War*, Dylan delivers a scathing indictment of the military-industrial complex, with lines like "You that build all the bombs / You that hide behind walls" expressing his anger and frustration in blunt, uncompromising terms. Dylan's courage in addressing these issues has made his music a powerful force for social change.

Ultimately, Bob Dylan's storytelling is about more than just recounting events—it's about exploring the human experience in all its complexity. His songs combine vivid imagery, rich characters, and layered narratives to create stories that feel both deeply personal and universally resonant. For songwriters, the lessons from Dylan's work are clear: embrace emotional honesty, use imagery to bring stories to life, and don't be afraid to tackle difficult or complex subjects. By doing so, you can create songs that not only tell compelling stories but also connect with listeners on a profound level.

Lessons from Van Morrison: Creating Atmosphere in Your Music

Van Morrison is a master of creating immersive atmospheres in his music, transporting listeners into vivid emotional and sensory worlds. His ability to combine poetic lyrics with rich instrumentation and soulful melodies makes his songs not just pieces of music, but experiences. From the mystical, ethereal landscapes of *Astral Weeks* to the nostalgic warmth of *Moondance*, Morrison's music teaches songwriters valuable lessons on how to evoke mood and atmosphere, making the listener feel like they're stepping into a different place or time.

One of the most powerful lessons from Van Morrison's work is the use of **imagery and sensory details** to create atmosphere. In songs like *Madame George* or *Into the Mystic*, Morrison paints pictures with his words, using vivid imagery to transport listeners into the world of the song. In *Into the Mystic*, for example, he writes: "We were born before the wind / Also younger than the sun / Ere the bonnie boat was won as we sailed into the mystic." These lines are not only poetic but evoke a dreamlike sense of wonder and exploration. By referencing natural elements like wind, sun, and the sea, Morrison grounds the song in sensory experiences that are deeply felt, not just heard.

For songwriters, this highlights the importance of **evoking the senses** to create an immersive atmosphere. Describing not just what a scene looks like but how it feels, sounds, and even smells can help to transport the listener. By tapping into sensory details, you allow the listener to experience the world of the song more fully. In *And It Stoned Me*, Morrison captures the feeling of youthful freedom with lines like "Oh the water, let it run all over me," grounding the story in the tactile sensations of nature and water, while also creating an atmosphere of nostalgia and innocence.

Another crucial aspect of Morrison's songwriting is his ability to **combine the mystical with the mundane**, blurring the lines between the spiritual and everyday life. In *Astral Weeks*, he sings about transcendence, longing, and spiritual awakening, but the imagery is grounded in everyday experiences: walking down streets, seeing people in windows, and feeling the passage of time. This mix of the mystical and the ordinary creates a unique atmosphere in Morrison's music—one that feels both rooted in the world and lifted beyond it. For songwriters, this approach offers a way to elevate simple stories or scenes by imbuing them with deeper meaning and emotion.

Morrison's use of **repetition and phrasing** is another essential tool in creating atmosphere. His songs often feature repeated lines or phrases that function almost like mantras, building a sense of emotional intensity or drawing the listener deeper into the mood of the song. In *Caravan*, the repeated refrain "Turn it up / Turn it up / Little bit higher, radio" not only serves as a call to action but also helps create the song's celebratory, communal atmosphere. The repetition becomes hypnotic, inviting the listener into the experience of being swept up by the music.

THIS USE OF REPETITION highlights the power of **simplicity in lyric writing**. Sometimes, the most evocative lines aren't the most complex or poetic but the ones that are repeated with conviction and emotion. Morrison's ability to use simple, repetitive phrases—whether it's "Into the mystic" or "Let your soul and spirit fly"—creates a sense of emotional layering, where the listener is pulled deeper into the atmosphere with each repetition. Songwriters can use this technique to build mood and reinforce the emotional core of a song, without overcomplicating the lyrics.

Van Morrison is also known for his **improvisational style**, which contributes to the spontaneous and organic feel of his music. His vocal delivery often feels free-flowing, almost as though he's discovering the song in real-time as he sings it. This gives his music an atmospheric looseness, where the listener feels like they're witnessing something unplanned and raw. In songs like *Cypress Avenue* or *Ballerina*, Morrison's phrasing and timing feel less constrained by structure and more driven by emotion, creating a sense of immediacy and presence.

For songwriters, this lesson is about letting go of rigid structures and embracing the **emotional flow of the song**. Instead of sticking strictly to a predetermined melody or rhythm, allow yourself to experiment with phrasing, timing, and vocal delivery. This can make your songs feel more organic and emotionally authentic, contributing to a stronger atmosphere. Improvisation also invites the listener into a more intimate space, as they experience the emotional shifts and changes along with you.

In terms of **instrumentation**, Morrison is a master of creating atmospheric soundscapes by blending genres and sounds in unexpected ways. His music often draws on a mix of jazz, folk, blues, and soul, with instrumentation that includes strings, horns, piano, and acoustic guitar. This eclectic mix of sounds contributes to the rich textures of his songs, giving them a layered, immersive quality. In *Moondance*, for example, the combination of jazzy piano chords, walking bass lines, and smooth saxophone solos creates a warm, laid-back atmosphere that feels like a nighttime stroll through a vibrant city.

For songwriters, the lesson here is to think about **how instrumentation can enhance the mood** of the song. The choice of instruments, the way they're arranged, and how they interact with each other can all play a big role in creating atmosphere. You don't need a complex arrangement to achieve this—sometimes a simple combination of acoustic guitar and a subtle string section can create an incredibly evocative mood. The key is to let the instrumentation serve the atmosphere you want to evoke. In *Into the Mystic*, the soft guitar strumming and warm horns perfectly match the song's themes of spiritual journey and reflection, giving it a serene, expansive feel.

Another way Morrison builds atmosphere is through **rhythmic variation** and **groove**. Many of his songs feature a loose, flowing rhythm that feels more like a natural pulse than a rigid beat. In *Moondance*, for instance, the smooth, swinging rhythm complements the song's playful, romantic lyrics. The relaxed tempo and jazz-inflected groove help create a dreamy, intimate atmosphere, inviting the listener to get lost in the song's laid-back vibe.

This teaches songwriters the importance of **matching rhythm to mood**. If you want to create an atmospheric, reflective song, a slower tempo or a more fluid, less structured rhythm might be more effective than a tight, fast-paced beat. By experimenting with the rhythm, you can reinforce the emotional tone of the song and create a deeper sense of atmosphere.

Morrison's use of **natural imagery and elements** is another key factor in creating the atmospheric quality of his music. Many of his songs reference the natural world—rivers, wind, mist, mountains, and skies—and these images help ground the emotional and spiritual themes in something tangible. In *Tupelo Honey*, for example, the recurring natural imagery ("She's as sweet as Tupelo honey / Just like honey from the bee") gives the song a sense of organic beauty and simplicity, creating a warm, comforting atmosphere.

For songwriters, the lesson is to think about how **nature and place** can be used to evoke specific emotions and settings. By referencing elements of the natural world, you can create a connection between the listener and the physical world of the song, making the atmosphere feel more real and immersive. Whether it's the misty, mystical setting of *Into the Mystic* or the golden autumn light of *Moondance*, Morrison's use of natural imagery makes the atmosphere of his songs feel grounded and expansive at the same time.

Finally, one of the most valuable lessons from Van Morrison is the importance of **emotional authenticity** in creating atmosphere. His music often feels deeply personal and spiritual, as though each song is an expression of his inner world. This authenticity is what makes his atmospheric music so powerful—it doesn't feel contrived or manufactured, but rather like a true reflection of his emotional state. Whether he's singing about love, nostalgia, or spiritual longing, Morrison's ability to convey real emotion is what makes the atmosphere of his music so compelling.

For songwriters, the takeaway is that atmosphere is not just about the technical elements—chords, instruments, or rhythm—but about how those elements are used to **convey genuine emotion**. When the emotional core of your song is real and deeply felt, the atmosphere will naturally follow. By focusing on emotional authenticity and allowing yourself to be vulnerable in your writing, you can create songs that resonate with listeners and transport them into the world of your music.

In conclusion, Van Morrison's music teaches songwriters how to create atmosphere through a combination of vivid imagery, emotional authenticity, improvisational flow, and thoughtful instrumentation. His ability to blend the mystical with the mundane, the spiritual with the everyday, gives his songs a timeless, immersive quality that continues to inspire listeners. By embracing these lessons, songwriters can learn to craft songs that not only tell stories but also create worlds for the listener to inhabit.

Lessons from Paul McCartney and John Lennon: The Perfect Songwriting Duo

Paul McCartney and John Lennon, as part of The Beatles, formed one of the most legendary songwriting partnerships in music history. Together, they created some of the most iconic songs of all time, blending their unique talents into a complementary force that redefined pop music. Their songwriting partnership offers many valuable lessons for songwriters, especially in terms of collaboration, creativity, and balance between contrasting styles. Though they often wrote separately in their later years, their early partnership and mutual influence remained crucial in shaping their individual styles and creating timeless music.

One of the most important lessons from McCartney and Lennon's partnership is the **power of collaboration**. While both were extraordinary songwriters in their own right, it was the push-and-pull of their partnership that often produced their best work. Their differences in musical style, personality, and approach to songwriting created a dynamic that allowed them to balance each other out. Lennon's lyrics tended to be more introspective, raw, and experimental, while McCartney had a knack for crafting melodic, upbeat, and accessible songs. Together, they blended Lennon's edge with McCartney's optimism, resulting in songs that had emotional depth and mass appeal.

For songwriters, this illustrates the value of **working with someone whose strengths complement your own**. Collaboration allows you to push beyond your comfort zone and explore ideas you might not have considered on your own. It also offers the opportunity to get feedback from someone who brings a different perspective. In the case of Lennon and McCartney, this dynamic can be seen in how they improved each other's songs. Lennon's raw, emotionally charged ideas were often polished and made more accessible by McCartney's melodic sensibilities, while McCartney's pop-focused ideas gained depth and texture from Lennon's lyrical introspection.

For example, in *A Day in the Life*, Lennon's darker, surreal verses are followed by McCartney's more optimistic and whimsical middle section, creating a contrast that gives the song its unique structure and atmosphere. This interplay between the two styles makes the song more layered and complex, illustrating how collaboration can take a song in unexpected directions. Songwriters can benefit from partnering with someone who challenges them creatively, helping to elevate the final product through contrasting strengths.

Another key lesson from McCartney and Lennon's partnership is the importance of **melodic and harmonic innovation**. One of the reasons their songs stand out is their inventive use of melody and harmony, often pushing the boundaries of traditional pop music. Songs like *Eleanor Rigby*, *Penny Lane*, and *Strawberry Fields Forever* showcase their ability to combine classical influences, unusual chord progressions, and inventive arrangements to create songs that were both innovative and emotionally resonant.

IN *Eleanor Rigby*, McCartney's use of string arrangements and a melody that veers away from typical pop structures gave the song a haunting, timeless quality. Meanwhile, Lennon's use of dreamy, dissonant chords in *Strawberry Fields Forever* created a surreal, psychedelic atmosphere. Both of these songs are examples of how Lennon and McCartney were not afraid to experiment with different musical ideas, giving their music depth and variety.

For songwriters, this highlights the value of **taking risks** with melody and harmony. While it's tempting to stick with familiar, comfortable progressions, pushing yourself to explore new chord changes, unusual melodies, or different genres can lead to more interesting and memorable songs. Lennon and McCartney's willingness to experiment is a reminder that great songwriting often comes from stepping outside of the norms and embracing innovation.

Their ability to **tell stories through lyrics** is another valuable lesson. Lennon and McCartney were not just great songwriters—they were great storytellers. Many of their songs tell vivid, character-driven stories that resonate with listeners on both a personal and emotional level. For example, *Eleanor Rigby* tells the tragic story of loneliness and isolation through the characters of Eleanor and Father McKenzie, while *She's Leaving Home* captures the emotional tension of a young girl leaving her family.

Both Lennon and McCartney excelled at creating characters and narratives that felt real and relatable, even when those stories were wrapped in surreal or abstract imagery. Lennon, in particular, often infused his lyrics with introspective and sometimes cryptic reflections on his own life, as in *In My Life*, while McCartney had a talent for capturing the everyday in a way that felt poignant and universal, as in *Penny Lane*.

Songwriters can learn from their storytelling approach by focusing on **narrative and character development** in their lyrics. Whether you're telling a specific story or capturing a broader emotional theme, developing characters and scenarios can make your songs more engaging and relatable. It's often the small, vivid details in Lennon and McCartney's lyrics that make their stories come to life.

One of the most striking aspects of their partnership was how they struck a balance between **personal expression and mass appeal**. Lennon's lyrics, especially later in his career, tended to be more autobiographical and introspective, dealing with his personal struggles, while McCartney had an innate ability to craft universally relatable songs. This balance is exemplified in songs like *Let It Be*—written by McCartney as a comforting tribute to his late mother—and *Nowhere Man*, where Lennon reflects on feelings of aimlessness and alienation.

For songwriters, the lesson is that it's possible to combine **personal experience with universal themes**. By writing from a personal place but connecting those emotions to something that resonates on a broader level, you can create songs that feel authentic and deeply impactful. Even when writing about something specific to your own life, there are ways to tap into emotions and experiences that listeners can relate to, allowing your personal stories to connect with a wider audience.

Another important takeaway from McCartney and Lennon's partnership is their use of **contrast and tension** in their songwriting. Many of their songs play with the contrast between light and dark, happy and sad, simple and complex. This dynamic tension is what gives their music depth and emotional resonance. For example, *We Can Work It Out* balances McCartney's optimistic verses ("We can work it out") with Lennon's more cynical perspective in the bridge ("Life is very short, and there's no time for fussing and fighting, my friend"). This push and pull between optimism and realism creates a more nuanced and layered song than if it had just leaned into one emotion.

Contrast can also be seen in their musical choices. In *Getting Better*, McCartney's upbeat, hopeful chorus ("It's getting better all the time") is tempered by Lennon's sardonic interjection ("It can't get no worse"), adding complexity to what might have been a straightforwardly positive song. For songwriters, this lesson is about **embracing complexity** in your work. By blending contrasting emotions, perspectives, or musical elements, you can create songs that feel more layered and emotionally rich.

Lennon and McCartney also show the value of **pushing each other to evolve creatively**. Over the course of their partnership, you can see how they influenced each other's growth as songwriters. Early on, they often wrote together, blending their ideas to create songs that were upbeat and energetic, like *I Want to Hold Your Hand* and *She Loves You*. As their careers progressed, both took on more individual roles in their songwriting, but the influence they had on each other remained strong. McCartney's knack for melody helped Lennon refine his approach to pop structures, while Lennon's more experimental and introspective tendencies encouraged McCartney to explore deeper emotional territory.

For songwriters, this is a reminder of the importance of **creative growth**. Collaborating with others, especially those who challenge you, can push you to try new things and develop your skills in unexpected ways. Even if you primarily write on your own, seeking out feedback and working with other musicians can help you evolve as a songwriter.

Finally, one of the key lessons from McCartney and Lennon is the importance of **adaptability and versatility**. Throughout their careers, they explored a wide range of genres, from rock and pop to folk, psychedelia, and even orchestral arrangements. This willingness to experiment with different styles and approaches kept their music fresh and exciting. For songwriters, it's a reminder that versatility is a valuable asset. Don't be afraid to step outside your comfort zone and try writing in different genres or experimenting with different sounds. By doing so, you'll discover new aspects of your creativity and keep your music evolving.

In conclusion, the songwriting partnership of Paul McCartney and John Lennon offers invaluable lessons for songwriters. From the power of collaboration and storytelling to the importance of contrast, innovation, and emotional depth, their work together showcases what's possible when two creative forces complement and challenge each other. By studying their approach, songwriters can learn how to balance personal expression with universal appeal, embrace risk and experimentation, and create songs that stand the test of time.

Lessons from Paul Simon: Blending Poetry and Melody

Paul Simon is one of the most gifted songwriters of his generation, known for his ability to blend poetic lyrics with memorable melodies. His songs, often introspective and rich in imagery, explore themes of love, loss, identity, and the human condition. Simon's songwriting is distinctive not only for its lyrical depth but also for its seamless integration of poetry and melody, creating songs that are emotionally resonant and musically captivating. His work offers valuable lessons for songwriters who seek to combine the art of lyrical storytelling with the craft of melody.

One of the most essential lessons from Paul Simon is the **importance of lyricism and poetry in songwriting**. Simon's lyrics are often filled with vivid imagery, metaphors, and wordplay, elevating his songs beyond simple narratives. In *The Sound of Silence*, for instance, Simon uses poetic language to explore themes of isolation, alienation, and communication. Lines like "People talking without speaking / People hearing without listening" reflect the complexity of human interaction in a way that feels both philosophical and emotionally impactful. This poetic approach invites listeners to interpret the song on multiple levels, making it more than just a catchy tune—it becomes an exploration of deeper meaning.

For songwriters, this highlights the power of **metaphor and symbolism** in lyrics. Rather than stating emotions or ideas directly, Simon often uses poetic devices to express abstract concepts in a way that resonates more deeply with the listener. In *America*, he writes, "The moon rose over an open field," using simple but evocative imagery to convey a sense of loneliness and searching. The landscape becomes a metaphor for the emotional and existential journey of the characters. Songwriters can learn from Simon's ability to **layer meaning in lyrics**, using poetic techniques to elevate their songs and give them more depth.

Another lesson from Paul Simon's songwriting is his ability to create **intimate, personal narratives** within his songs, often combining the poetic with the personal in ways that feel authentic and emotionally raw. Many of Simon's songs tell stories that feel both specific and universal, allowing listeners to connect with them on a personal level. In *Graceland*, for example, Simon tells the story of a man on a pilgrimage to the home of Elvis Presley, but the song is also about loss, recovery, and redemption. The lines "Losing love is like a window in your heart / Everybody sees you're blown apart" capture the emotional devastation of heartbreak in a way that feels deeply personal yet universally relatable.

For songwriters, this demonstrates the power of **personal storytelling**. While Simon's lyrics are often poetic, they are also grounded in human experience, allowing listeners to see themselves in the stories he tells. By drawing on personal emotions and experiences, but presenting them in a way that resonates broadly, you can create songs that feel both intimate and accessible. This is a delicate balance that Simon masters—he writes from a personal place, but his songs transcend the specific details to speak to larger truths about the human condition.

PAUL SIMON IS ALSO known for his **musical versatility**, which plays a significant role in how his lyrics and melodies interact. Over his career, Simon has explored a wide range of musical styles, from folk and rock to jazz, reggae, and world music influences, particularly African and Latin rhythms. This willingness to experiment with different genres has allowed him to find the perfect musical setting for his lyrics, ensuring that the melody enhances the emotional tone of the song. In *You Can Call Me Al*, the playful, upbeat melody and infectious rhythm contrast with the more introspective lyrics about identity and midlife crisis, creating a song that is both fun and thought-provoking.

For songwriters, the lesson here is the importance of **matching melody and music to the emotional content of the lyrics**. While Simon often experiments with diverse musical styles, his melodies always serve the story of the song. The buoyant, world-music-infused melodies of *Graceland* amplify the themes of personal and emotional journeys, while the haunting, minimalist melody of *The Sound of Silence* reinforces its themes of isolation and disconnectedness. By being intentional about the relationship between melody and lyrics, songwriters can create a more cohesive and emotionally impactful experience.

Simon's use of **rhythm and phrasing** is another defining feature of his songwriting. He often plays with unconventional phrasing, fitting his lyrics into rhythmic patterns that feel both natural and conversational, even when they stray from traditional song structures. In *Me and Julio Down by the Schoolyard*, Simon uses playful, syncopated rhythms to give the song a breezy, carefree feel, even as the lyrics remain somewhat cryptic. This rhythmic experimentation gives his songs a unique flow, where the melody and lyrics feel intertwined in a way that feels both loose and precise.

For songwriters, this demonstrates the importance of **rhythmic flexibility** in songwriting. While it's tempting to stick to familiar rhythms and structures, Simon's music shows that breaking free from rigid patterns can lead to more dynamic and interesting songs. Experimenting with different phrasing, syncopation, and rhythmic structures allows you to create melodies that feel fresh and spontaneous, while also giving your lyrics room to breathe and unfold naturally.

Another hallmark of Simon's songwriting is his ability to blend **melancholy with hope** in his lyrics and melodies. Many of his songs explore themes of loss, longing, and existential reflection, yet they often leave room for optimism or redemption. In *Bridge Over Troubled Water*, for instance, the lyrics speak to the pain and struggles of life, but the soaring, hopeful melody provides comfort and reassurance. The combination of melancholy lyrics and uplifting music creates a powerful emotional contrast, making the song feel deeply moving and cathartic.

For songwriters, this demonstrates the value of **emotional complexity** in songwriting. Rather than writing songs that are purely happy or sad, Simon often blends different emotions to create songs that feel layered and real. This emotional complexity allows listeners to experience a range of feelings within a single song, making the music more relatable and impactful. By blending contrasting emotions—such as hope and despair, joy and sorrow—you can create songs that feel more authentic and resonate on a deeper level.

Simon's use of **collaborations and influences** is another valuable lesson for songwriters. Over his career, Simon has worked with a wide range of musicians and drawn on diverse musical traditions, particularly during the creation of *Graceland*, which was heavily influenced by South African music. These collaborations not only expanded Simon's musical palette but also enriched his songwriting, allowing him to explore new rhythms, harmonies, and textures that complemented his poetic lyrics.

For songwriters, this illustrates the importance of **being open to collaboration and outside influences**. Working with musicians from different genres or cultures can inspire new creative ideas and bring fresh perspectives to your songwriting. Collaborations can also challenge you to step outside your comfort zone and explore new musical approaches that you might not have considered on your own. Simon's work shows that by embracing different influences, you can push the boundaries of your music and create songs that feel innovative and timeless.

One final lesson from Paul Simon's songwriting is his **attention to detail** in both lyrics and music. Simon is known for his meticulous approach to songwriting, often spending long periods refining his lyrics and melodies until they perfectly align. His songs are carefully crafted, with each word, note, and rhythm serving a specific purpose. This attention to detail is evident in songs like *The Boxer*, where the lyrics are finely honed to tell a vivid, emotionally charged story, and the arrangement is layered with subtle instrumentation that enhances the song's mood.

For songwriters, this underscores the importance of **patience and precision** in the creative process. While inspiration often strikes quickly, great songs often require time, revision, and careful consideration to fully take shape. By paying attention to the details—whether it's finding the perfect word, melody, or chord progression—you can create songs that feel polished and complete, without losing their emotional impact.

In conclusion, Paul Simon's ability to blend poetry and melody offers songwriters a wealth of lessons. From his use of vivid imagery and metaphor to his mastery of rhythm and phrasing, Simon's work demonstrates how lyrics and music can work together to create songs that are emotionally resonant and musically captivating. By drawing on personal experiences, experimenting with musical styles, and embracing collaboration, songwriters can learn to craft songs that are both deeply personal and universally relatable. Simon's meticulous approach to songwriting also reminds us of the value of patience, precision, and attention to detail in the pursuit of creating timeless music.

Lessons from Sting: Crafting Songs with Complexity and Simplicity

S ting, both as a member of The Police and as a solo artist, has built a reputation as a master songwriter who effortlessly combines musical complexity with lyrical simplicity. His ability to blend intricate musical arrangements with clear, emotionally resonant lyrics offers valuable lessons for songwriters striving to balance artistic sophistication with accessibility. Sting's work draws from a wide range of influences, including jazz, reggae, classical music, and rock, and he skillfully layers these diverse elements without overwhelming the listener. His songs are a masterclass in how to craft music that is at once deeply complex and strikingly simple.

One of the most important lessons from Sting is how to **embrace musical complexity** without sacrificing the core emotional appeal of the song. Sting's music often features unusual time signatures, intricate chord progressions, and advanced harmonic structures. For example, *Englishman in New York* is built on a jazz-inspired melody with syncopated rhythms and harmonic complexity, yet it remains accessible because the melody is memorable and the lyrical theme is relatable. The complexity serves the song, adding texture and sophistication without detracting from its emotional impact.

For songwriters, this shows that it's possible to explore **musical innovation** while still maintaining clarity and emotional resonance. Rather than shying away from complex musical ideas, Sting integrates them in a way that enhances the song's narrative and emotional tone. The lesson here is not to overcomplicate a song for complexity's sake but to use complexity to elevate the music. Whether it's through a creative time signature, a surprising chord change, or an unexpected melodic twist, these elements can make a song more engaging and layered.

At the same time, Sting demonstrates the power of **simplicity in lyrics**. While his music is often harmonically complex, his lyrics tend to be straightforward and emotionally direct. In *Every Breath You Take*, for instance, the melody is built around a repetitive chord progression, but the lyrics, which describe obsession and heartbreak, are simple and universally understood. The repetitive nature of both the melody and the lyrics drives home the emotional intensity of the song, showing that even a basic structure can be incredibly powerful when it's paired with the right emotional content.

For songwriters, the lesson is that **lyrical simplicity** can be just as effective as musical complexity. Sometimes, less is more when it comes to lyrics, especially when the music is doing a lot of the emotional heavy lifting. By stripping the lyrics down to their most essential elements, as Sting often does, you allow the listener to focus on the core message of the song without getting lost in overly ornate language.

Sting also shows the importance of **contrasting complexity and simplicity** within a song. In *Fields of Gold*, for example, the lyrics are poetic but straightforward, telling a story of love and nostalgia in a way that feels both personal and universal. The melody and chord progression are relatively simple, but the arrangement—featuring lush strings, soft guitar, and Sting's gentle vocal delivery—adds layers of emotional depth. This balance between the simplicity of the melody and the complexity of the arrangement creates a song that feels rich and emotionally resonant, without being overwhelming.

For songwriters, this approach is a reminder that **contrast** can be a powerful tool. By pairing a simple, singable melody with a more complex arrangement, you can create a song that feels both accessible and sophisticated. Conversely, you can use a more intricate melody or chord progression and balance it with simple lyrics or a minimalist arrangement to achieve a similar effect. The key is to find the right balance between complexity and simplicity so that they complement each other, rather than compete for attention.

Another lesson from Sting's songwriting is his ability to **incorporate diverse musical influences** while maintaining a cohesive sound. Throughout his career, Sting has drawn from a wide range of genres, including reggae, jazz, classical music, and world music. In *Roxanne*, for instance, he blends elements of reggae with rock, creating a unique sound that was groundbreaking at the time. In *Shape of My Heart*, Sting incorporates classical guitar and jazz-influenced harmonies, resulting in a song that feels both timeless and contemporary.

For songwriters, this shows the value of being **open to different musical styles and influences**. Sting's willingness to explore various genres and incorporate them into his own music gives his work a sense of depth and variety that keeps it fresh and interesting. By experimenting with different musical styles—whether it's borrowing rhythms from reggae, harmonies from jazz, or melodies from classical music—you can expand your musical palette and create songs that feel unique and original.

Sting's attention to **rhythm and groove** is another important aspect of his songwriting. Many of his most iconic songs, like *Message in a Bottle* and *Walking on the Moon*, are built around infectious grooves and rhythmic patterns that give the music its energy and momentum. Sting often uses syncopation and off-beat rhythms to create a sense of tension and release, drawing the listener in and keeping them engaged. This rhythmic complexity is a hallmark of Sting's music, but it's always balanced by strong melodic lines and accessible lyrics.

For songwriters, the lesson here is to pay attention to **rhythm as a central element** of the song. A well-crafted rhythm can drive a song forward, making it more dynamic and compelling. Even if your melody and lyrics are relatively simple, an interesting rhythm or groove can elevate the entire song. Sting's music shows that rhythm isn't just a background element—it's an essential part of the songwriting process that can make a song more memorable and engaging.

Sting's use of **themes and storytelling** in his lyrics is another lesson for songwriters. Many of his songs explore deep, often philosophical themes, such as identity, love, mortality, and human connection. In *Fragile*, for example, Sting reflects on violence and the fragility of life with simple but poignant lyrics: "If blood will flow when flesh and steel are one / Drying in the color of the evening sun." The song's quiet, haunting melody complements the gravity of the theme, creating a powerful emotional impact.

For songwriters, this demonstrates the power of **thematic depth** in lyrics. Sting's songs often work on multiple levels, combining personal emotions with broader, universal themes. By exploring larger ideas—such as love, loss, or social issues—through the lens of personal experience, you can create songs that resonate with listeners on a deeper level. Sting's approach shows that even a simple song can carry a profound message when the lyrics are thoughtful and reflective.

Another important aspect of Sting's songwriting is his **emotional honesty**. Whether he's singing about love, loss, or existential questions, Sting's lyrics feel authentic and heartfelt. This emotional authenticity is one of the reasons his songs resonate so strongly with listeners. In *If I Ever Lose My Faith in You*, for instance, Sting expresses feelings of disillusionment and uncertainty, but also leaves room for hope and redemption. The honesty in his lyrics allows listeners to connect with the song on a personal level, even if their experiences are different.

For songwriters, this highlights the importance of **vulnerability and emotional truth** in songwriting. Being open and honest in your lyrics—even when dealing with complex or difficult emotions—allows listeners to relate to the song on a deeper level. Sting's music shows that when you write from a place of emotional authenticity, your songs will resonate with listeners, no matter how simple or complex the music might be.

Sting's **song structures** are another valuable lesson for songwriters. While many of his songs follow traditional verse-chorus structures, he often adds unexpected twists, such as key changes, extended instrumental sections, or shifts in time signature. This willingness to play with form keeps his music interesting and unpredictable, without losing its sense of cohesion. In *Russians*, for instance, Sting uses a minor key and a classical-inspired melody to create a sense of tension and drama, while the structure of the song builds steadily toward its emotional climax.

For songwriters, this demonstrates the value of **experimenting with song structure**. While traditional forms can be effective, breaking away from them occasionally can create a more dynamic and engaging listening experience. Whether it's by adding a bridge, extending a chorus, or changing the key, experimenting with structure can help you keep your songs fresh and compelling.

In conclusion, Sting's ability to craft songs that balance complexity and simplicity offers valuable lessons for songwriters. From his use of intricate rhythms and harmonies to his emotionally direct lyrics, Sting shows how music can be both sophisticated and accessible. By embracing musical experimentation, paying attention to rhythm and groove, and writing with emotional honesty, songwriters can create songs that resonate deeply with listeners while still pushing the boundaries of what's possible in music. Whether working with complex arrangements or simple melodies, Sting's approach reminds us that the heart of a great song lies in its ability to connect with the listener on an emotional level.

Lessons from Neil Diamond: Emotion and Simplicity in Songwriting

Neil Diamond is a master of crafting songs that connect with listeners on an emotional level through simple, yet deeply resonant lyrics and melodies. His ability to take universal themes—love, heartbreak, hope, and perseverance—and express them with clarity and feeling has made him one of the most successful and enduring songwriters of all time. Diamond's songs are often built around simple structures, but it's the raw emotion, sincerity, and straightforward delivery that make them powerful. For songwriters, Diamond's work offers essential lessons in how to convey deep emotions with simplicity and grace.

One of the most important lessons from Neil Diamond's songwriting is the power of **emotional honesty**. Diamond's lyrics are often direct and unpretentious, speaking to fundamental human emotions in a way that feels genuine and relatable. In songs like *I Am... I Said*, he expresses feelings of loneliness and inner conflict with striking simplicity: "I am, I said / To no one there / And no one heard at all / Not even the chair." These lines are deceptively simple, but they convey a profound sense of isolation and yearning. The lack of embellishment allows the emotional truth of the lyrics to shine through, making the song deeply moving.

For songwriters, this demonstrates the value of **keeping lyrics clear and emotionally direct**. Rather than relying on complex metaphors or abstract imagery, Diamond's lyrics often cut straight to the heart of the matter. This approach makes his songs more accessible to listeners, who can easily relate to the emotions being expressed. The lesson here is that sometimes the simplest way to convey an emotion is also the most effective. By stripping away unnecessary complexity, you can create songs that speak directly to the listener's feelings and experiences.

Diamond also excels at **building songs around universal themes**, which contributes to their wide appeal. Many of his songs explore themes that everyone can relate to—love, loneliness, desire, and hope. In *Sweet Caroline*, for example, Diamond taps into the joy and warmth of a shared moment of affection with lyrics like "Good times never seemed so good." The simplicity of the sentiment is what makes it so powerful; it captures a universally understood feeling and expresses it in a way that's easy for listeners to connect with.

For songwriters, this highlights the importance of **writing about emotions and experiences that are widely relatable**. By focusing on universal themes, you can create songs that resonate with a broad audience. Whether you're writing about love, heartbreak, or perseverance, the key is to express these emotions in a way that feels authentic and true to your own experiences. Diamond's songs often reflect his personal emotions, but they do so in a way that feels universal, allowing listeners to see themselves in the lyrics.

ANOTHER IMPORTANT ASPECT of Neil Diamond's songwriting is his **use of melody to enhance the emotional impact of the lyrics**. Diamond's melodies are often simple and memorable, allowing the emotion of the lyrics to take center stage. In *Song Sung Blue*, for instance, the melody is straightforward and repetitive, mirroring the theme of the song—a reflection on sadness and finding comfort in music. The simplicity of the melody makes the song feel familiar and comforting, which reinforces the emotional message.

For songwriters, the lesson here is to **create melodies that support and amplify the emotion of the song**. While it can be tempting to write complex or intricate melodies, sometimes the most effective approach is to keep it simple and let the emotional weight of the lyrics carry the song. A strong, memorable melody can make a song more impactful by reinforcing the emotional tone and making it easier for listeners to engage with the music.

Diamond's songs often make use of **repetition**, both in melody and lyrics, to create emotional depth and resonance. In *America*, the repeated refrain "They're coming to America" builds a sense of anticipation and hope, while the simple, driving melody reinforces the song's message of optimism and perseverance. The repetition of key phrases and musical motifs helps to create a sense of unity and emotional continuity throughout the song.

For songwriters, this demonstrates the power of **repetition in songwriting**. Repeating certain phrases or melodies can help to reinforce the emotional core of the song and make it more memorable. However, it's important to use repetition intentionally, ensuring that it serves the emotional narrative of the song. Diamond's use of repetition is never excessive; it's always carefully placed to heighten the emotional impact and keep the listener engaged.

Another valuable lesson from Neil Diamond is his ability to **write anthemic, singable choruses**. Many of Diamond's most famous songs, such as *Sweet Caroline* and *Cracklin' Rosie*, feature choruses that are easy to sing along to, making the songs feel communal and uplifting. The choruses are often built around simple, repetitive melodies and lyrics that invite participation. This makes the songs feel like shared experiences, where listeners are encouraged to join in and connect with the music on a more personal level.

For songwriters, the lesson here is to **craft choruses that are both emotionally resonant and singable**. A great chorus doesn't need to be complex or lyrically dense—it needs to be something that listeners can latch onto and feel compelled to sing along with. The emotional simplicity of Diamond's choruses, combined with their catchy melodies, is what makes them so powerful. When writing your own choruses, focus on creating something that feels emotionally direct and musically inviting, encouraging listeners to engage with the song on a deeper level.

Diamond's use of **storytelling in songwriting** is another key aspect of his success. Many of his songs tell stories that are emotionally rich and relatable, often focusing on personal journeys or reflections. In *Brooklyn Roads*, Diamond reflects on his childhood and the passage of time, using specific details to paint a vivid picture of his experiences: "I walked to the hill / To watch the sun go down / And from there I'd see the places / Where we used to run." The personal nature of the song gives it emotional weight, while the storytelling structure makes it engaging and relatable.

For songwriters, this illustrates the value of **personal storytelling in lyrics**. Writing from your own experiences or drawing on personal memories can create songs that feel authentic and emotionally grounded. By sharing personal stories in your lyrics, you allow listeners to connect with your music on a more intimate level, making the songs more meaningful and impactful.

One of the most remarkable things about Neil Diamond's songwriting is his ability to **balance simplicity with depth**. While his songs often feature simple melodies and lyrics, they are never shallow or lacking in emotional complexity. Diamond's ability to convey deep emotions through straightforward language and accessible melodies is what makes his music so powerful. In *Love on the Rocks*, for example, the lyrics are simple and direct, but they convey a profound sense of heartache: "Love on the rocks, ain't no surprise / Pour me a drink and I'll tell you some lies." The simplicity of the language allows the raw emotion to come through, making the song feel both personal and universal.

For songwriters, the lesson here is to **embrace emotional simplicity without sacrificing depth**. It's possible to write songs that are both easy to understand and emotionally complex by focusing on the core emotions and experiences that drive the song. Diamond's ability to express deep feelings with simple words and melodies is a testament to the power of emotional clarity in songwriting.

Another key aspect of Diamond's songwriting is his use of **strong, clear song structures**. His songs often follow familiar verse-chorus structures, but within that framework, he finds ways to build emotional intensity and momentum. In *Hello Again*, for example, the song builds gradually, with each verse adding emotional weight until the climactic chorus delivers a powerful release of emotion. The clear structure allows the listener to follow the emotional arc of the song, making the journey feel satisfying and complete.

For songwriters, this highlights the importance of **using structure to enhance the emotional impact** of the song. While it's important to experiment and find your own voice, using clear structures can help you guide the listener through the emotional journey of the song. A well-crafted structure provides a foundation for the melody and lyrics, allowing the emotional narrative to unfold naturally.

In conclusion, Neil Diamond's songwriting offers valuable lessons for any songwriter looking to create music that connects emotionally with listeners. From his use of simplicity in lyrics and melody to his ability to tell personal stories and convey universal emotions, Diamond's work demonstrates the power of emotional clarity and directness in songwriting. By focusing on core emotions, crafting singable choruses, and using repetition and structure to reinforce the song's emotional message, songwriters can learn to create songs that are both deeply personal and widely relatable. Diamond's music reminds us that sometimes the most powerful songs are the ones that speak directly to the heart, with honesty, simplicity, and emotional resonance.

Lessons from The Eagles: Harmonizing Melody and Lyric

The Eagles are renowned for their masterful harmonies, timeless melodies, and storytelling lyrics. Their ability to blend these elements seamlessly has made them one of the most successful and influential bands in rock history. The Eagles' songwriting, often a collaborative effort between members like Don Henley, Glenn Frey, and others, offers valuable lessons for any songwriter seeking to harmonize melody and lyric, while crafting songs that resonate emotionally and musically. The Eagles' music combines emotional depth with melodic richness, providing a template for how to create songs that are both lyrically meaningful and musically captivating.

One of the most significant lessons from The Eagles is their **use of vocal harmonies** to enhance the emotional power of a song. The band's harmonies are often rich and intricate, adding texture and depth to even the simplest melodies. In songs like *Take It Easy* and *Seven Bridges Road*, the harmonized vocals create a sense of unity and fullness that makes the music more immersive. The harmonies are not just decorative—they serve to underscore the emotional content of the lyrics, making the songs feel more powerful and resonant.

For songwriters, this highlights the importance of **harmonizing not just the melody, but also the emotions** in the lyrics. Vocal harmonies can be used to reinforce the mood of a song, whether it's adding warmth and support in a hopeful track, or creating tension in a more introspective or darker piece. Harmonies also give the music a sense of grandeur, which can help elevate the song's emotional impact. By thinking about how harmonies can support the emotional narrative of your song, you can add an extra layer of depth to your music.

Another key lesson from The Eagles is their **focus on storytelling through lyrics**. Many of their most iconic songs, like *Hotel California*, *Desperado*, and *Lyin' Eyes*, tell vivid, character-driven stories that capture the listener's imagination. In *Hotel California*, the lyrics paint a haunting picture of a mysterious, seductive place that symbolizes excess, temptation, and the inability to escape one's choices. The imagery is both specific and open to interpretation, allowing listeners to draw their own conclusions while being drawn into the narrative.

For songwriters, this demonstrates the power of **storytelling in lyrics**. The Eagles often use their songs to tell stories, whether they are about personal relationships, societal issues, or emotional struggles. This storytelling approach gives their songs a sense of depth and purpose, making them more engaging for the listener. When writing lyrics, consider how you can use narrative and character to draw listeners into the world of the song. Whether it's a literal story or a more metaphorical journey, storytelling can make your lyrics more memorable and impactful.

The Eagles also excel at **blending melody and lyrics** in a way that feels organic and natural. Their melodies often complement the lyrical themes, creating a cohesive musical experience. In *Desperado*, for example, the somber, piano-driven melody perfectly matches the reflective, melancholy tone of the lyrics, which explore themes of loneliness and the longing for redemption. The melody and lyrics work together to create a unified emotional landscape, where the music amplifies the message of the words.

For songwriters, the lesson is to **ensure that the melody and lyrics are in harmony**, not just musically, but emotionally. The melody should reflect and enhance the mood and message of the lyrics. If the lyrics are expressing sadness or introspection, the melody should support that feeling rather than contradict it. Conversely, if the lyrics are hopeful or celebratory, the melody can reinforce that optimism. By paying attention to the emotional alignment between melody and lyrics, you can create songs that feel more cohesive and impactful.

One of The Eagles' greatest strengths is their **ability to write relatable lyrics** that connect with a wide audience. Their songs often explore universal themes—love, betrayal, freedom, and regret—in ways that feel both personal and accessible. In *Lyin' Eyes*, the lyrics tell the story of a woman trapped in an unfulfilling relationship, but the emotions of deception and longing are something many listeners can relate to. The specific story becomes a vehicle for expressing broader emotional truths, making the song resonate on multiple levels.

For songwriters, this emphasizes the importance of **finding the universal in the personal**. Even if you're writing about a specific experience or relationship, focusing on the emotions at the core of the story can make the song relatable to a broader audience. The Eagles' ability to write lyrics that speak to common human experiences is one of the reasons their music has such lasting appeal. By tapping into emotions that listeners can identify with, you can create songs that feel more meaningful and resonant.

Another valuable lesson from The Eagles is their **use of musical dynamics** to build emotional intensity. Many of their songs start with a simple, stripped-down arrangement and gradually build in complexity and intensity as the song progresses. In *Hotel California*, for example, the song begins with a mellow, acoustic guitar riff, but as the narrative unfolds, the music builds in intensity, culminating in an iconic, climactic guitar solo. This dynamic build mirrors the growing tension in the lyrics, creating a sense of drama and emotional release.

For songwriters, this shows the power of **using dynamics to tell a story**. By starting with a simple arrangement and gradually adding layers of instrumentation, you can create a sense of progression and development in the song. This technique keeps the listener engaged, as the music evolves along with the emotional arc of the lyrics. Using dynamics to build tension and then release it can make the emotional journey of the song more impactful.

The Eagles also teach the importance of **collaboration in songwriting**. Much of their success came from the collaboration between Don Henley and Glenn Frey, who wrote many of the band's biggest hits together. Each brought different strengths to the table—Henley's introspective, often melancholic lyrics balanced Frey's more upbeat, melodic sensibilities. Their collaboration created a dynamic balance between light and dark, making their songs emotionally complex and layered.

For songwriters, this demonstrates the value of **working with others to enhance your creative process**. Collaborating with another songwriter or musician can bring fresh perspectives to your work and push you to explore new ideas. The Eagles' success as a band is a testament to the power of creative partnerships, where different strengths and ideas can combine to create something greater than the sum of its parts.

Another lesson from The Eagles is their **focus on craftsmanship and attention to detail**. Their songs are meticulously arranged, with each instrument and vocal part carefully considered to create a polished, cohesive sound. Whether it's the intricate guitar work on *Hotel California* or the layered harmonies on *Peaceful Easy Feeling*, the band's attention to detail is evident in every note.

For songwriters, this highlights the importance of **being deliberate in your arrangements and production**. Even if you're writing a simple acoustic song, thinking carefully about how each element contributes to the overall sound can make a big difference. The Eagles' music shows that great songs aren't just about great melodies or lyrics—they're about how all the elements come together to create a cohesive, polished whole.

Finally, The Eagles demonstrate the importance of **staying true to your musical identity**. Throughout their career, they remained committed to their signature blend of rock, country, and folk influences, even as musical trends changed around them. This consistency helped them build a strong, enduring connection with their audience. While their sound evolved over time, they never strayed too far from the core elements that defined their music—harmonies, storytelling lyrics, and rich, melodic arrangements.

For songwriters, this is a reminder to **stay true to your own voice and style**. While it's important to grow and evolve as an artist, it's equally important to hold onto the elements that make your music unique. The Eagles' success shows that when you remain authentic to your sound and vision, your music will resonate with listeners in a deeper and more lasting way.

In conclusion, The Eagles offer songwriters invaluable lessons in harmonizing melody and lyric. From their use of vocal harmonies and storytelling lyrics to their focus on emotional alignment between melody and words, The Eagles show how to craft songs that are both musically and emotionally compelling. Their attention to detail, mastery of dynamics, and collaborative spirit further highlight the importance of crafting songs with care and intention. By learning from their approach, songwriters can create music that resonates deeply with listeners, balancing simplicity with sophistication and melody with meaning.

Lessons from Kurt Cobain: Raw Emotion and Defying Convention in Songwriting

Kurt Cobain, the frontman of Nirvana, is widely regarded as one of the most influential songwriters of the 1990s, and his legacy continues to resonate in music today. His work was raw, visceral, and unpolished, often reflecting the angst and alienation of Generation X, yet it struck a chord with a global audience. Cobain's ability to capture complex emotions in deceptively simple lyrics and melodies, combined with his rejection of conventional songwriting structures, offers invaluable lessons for songwriters who want to create music that feels genuine, emotionally charged, and defies expectations.

One of the most important lessons from Kurt Cobain is the **power of raw emotion in songwriting**. Cobain's lyrics were often abstract, filled with fragmented thoughts and surreal imagery, but they conveyed intense, often overwhelming emotions. In songs like *Smells Like Teen Spirit* and *Heart-Shaped Box*, Cobain taps into a sense of frustration, confusion, and vulnerability that resonated deeply with listeners. His voice—both literal and lyrical—was unpolished, and that lack of perfection is what made his music feel so authentic.

For songwriters, this is a reminder that **emotional authenticity** is often more powerful than technical precision. Cobain didn't aim for polished, radio-friendly songs; instead, he embraced the imperfections in his voice and playing, allowing the rawness of his feelings to shine through. The lesson here is that it's okay to let your guard down in your songwriting. Embracing your vulnerabilities, expressing frustration, sadness, or confusion without trying to "perfect" it, can create a deep connection with listeners who relate to those emotions.

Cobain also defied many of the **traditional rules of songwriting**, particularly when it came to structure and melody. Nirvana's music often combined catchy, almost pop-like melodies with aggressive, distorted guitar riffs and screamed vocals, creating a contrast that was both jarring and exhilarating. *Smells Like Teen Spirit* is a prime example of this blend—its verse-chorus structure is familiar and accessible, but the way Cobain plays with dynamics, going from quiet, subdued verses to explosive, loud choruses, creates a sense of unpredictability that was fresh and exciting.

For songwriters, this teaches the importance of **embracing contrast** in your music. Cobain's songs often built tension by alternating between soft and loud, simple and chaotic. This dynamic contrast made his music feel unpredictable and emotionally charged. Whether it's in the arrangement, the melody, or the lyrics, finding ways to introduce contrast can make your songs more engaging. You don't need to stick to one mood or style throughout a song—explore different dynamics and see how they can amplify the emotional impact of your music.

Cobain's lyrics were famously **ambiguous and abstract**, yet they still conveyed deep meaning. He often wrote in a stream-of-consciousness style, using fragmented images and seemingly disjointed phrases to create a mood or atmosphere. In songs like *Come As You Are* and *All Apologies*, the lyrics are open to interpretation, allowing listeners to bring their own experiences and emotions to the music. This lyrical ambiguity gave Cobain's songs a universal appeal, despite their intensely personal origins.

For songwriters, this highlights the power of **leaving space for interpretation**. Not every song needs to tell a clear, linear story; sometimes, ambiguous or abstract lyrics can evoke stronger emotions because they allow listeners to find their own meaning. Cobain's lyrics often felt like puzzle pieces—he provided the emotional framework, but listeners were free to interpret them in their own way. When writing your own lyrics, don't be afraid to be abstract or cryptic—sometimes, less clarity can lead to more emotional depth.

Another key lesson from Cobain is his use of **simple, repetitive chord progressions** to create powerful, emotionally resonant songs. Nirvana's music often featured basic, straightforward chord progressions, but it was the way Cobain played those chords—with intensity and emotional conviction—that made them impactful. In *Smells Like Teen Spirit*, the four-chord progression is simple, but the energy and aggression with which it's played transform it into something much more powerful.

For songwriters, this demonstrates that **simplicity can be powerful** when combined with emotional conviction. You don't need complex chord progressions or intricate arrangements to create a song that resonates with listeners. Sometimes, a simple melody or chord structure, when played with passion and intensity, can be just as impactful as something more technically complex. The key is to put your heart into it—if you believe in the emotion behind the song, the simplicity of the music can amplify that feeling.

Cobain's songwriting was also characterized by a **deep sense of rebellion and defiance**. He frequently rejected mainstream musical trends and societal norms, both in his lyrics and his approach to music. Songs like *Lithium* and *In Bloom* challenge conventional ideas about identity, conformity, and mental health, often with a sense of irony or dark humor. Cobain wasn't afraid to confront uncomfortable topics or criticize the culture around him, and this rebellious spirit made his music feel urgent and relevant.

For songwriters, this is a reminder to **stay true to your artistic vision** and not shy away from difficult or controversial topics. Cobain's willingness to challenge societal norms and express uncomfortable truths is part of what made his music so impactful. When writing your own songs, don't be afraid to take risks or address topics that may be considered taboo or unconventional. Music has the power to provoke thought and stir emotions, and by embracing a rebellious or defiant spirit, you can create songs that feel more authentic and powerful.

Another defining element of Cobain's songwriting was his **ability to capture the feeling of alienation and disillusionment** that many listeners, particularly young people, could relate to. His lyrics often reflected a sense of not fitting in, feeling disconnected from society, or struggling with inner turmoil. In *Something in the Way*, Cobain paints a bleak picture of isolation and despair, using sparse instrumentation and haunting lyrics to evoke a powerful emotional response.

FOR SONGWRITERS, THIS shows the value of **writing about emotions that people can relate to, even if those emotions are difficult or painful**. Cobain's music resonated with listeners because he was unafraid to explore themes of depression, isolation, and confusion—feelings that many people experience but often struggle to express. By writing about your own emotional struggles, you can create songs that connect with listeners on a deeply personal level. Cobain's ability to tap into those darker emotions without sugarcoating them is one of the reasons his music has had such a lasting impact.

Cobain's songwriting also benefited from his **distinctive voice and delivery**. His voice was raw, imperfect, and often strained, but that imperfection became part of his signature sound. Cobain's vocal delivery was filled with emotional intensity—whether he was singing softly or screaming at the top of his lungs, there was always a sense of urgency and authenticity in his voice. His vocal style, much like his lyrics, wasn't polished or refined, but it was deeply expressive.

For songwriters, this demonstrates the importance of **embracing your unique voice**. You don't need to have a "perfect" singing voice or follow conventional standards of vocal performance to create impactful music. What matters most is the emotional sincerity in your delivery. Cobain's voice was powerful because it conveyed real emotion, and listeners could feel that honesty. When performing your own songs, focus on delivering the lyrics in a way that feels true to the emotion behind them, even if your voice isn't traditionally perfect.

Finally, Kurt Cobain's songwriting teaches the value of **staying true to your artistic instincts**, even in the face of pressure to conform to commercial expectations. Cobain never set out to create mainstream music, yet Nirvana's success propelled him into the spotlight. Despite this, he remained committed to his artistic vision, continuing to write songs that reflected his personal struggles and defied the expectations of the industry. This authenticity is part of what made Cobain such a revered figure in music.

For songwriters, the lesson is to **stay true to your creative instincts** and not compromise your vision for the sake of commercial success. Cobain's music resonated with people because it was genuine and unapologetically raw. While commercial success can be a goal, the most powerful songs are often those that come from a place of honesty and artistic integrity.

In conclusion, Kurt Cobain's songwriting offers invaluable lessons for songwriters who want to create music that feels raw, authentic, and emotionally resonant. From his use of simplicity and ambiguity in lyrics to his embrace of imperfection and defiance of convention, Cobain's work demonstrates the power of emotional sincerity in music. By staying true to your voice, writing about difficult emotions, and embracing the imperfections in your craft, you can create songs that connect with listeners on a profound level, just as Cobain's music continues to do decades after his passing.

Lessons from Burt Bacharach: Mastering Melody, Harmony, and Emotion in Songwriting

Burt Bacharach was one of the most iconic and influential songwriters of the 20th century, known for his sophisticated melodies, innovative harmonic progressions, and emotionally rich compositions. With a career that spanned decades and numerous hit songs, Bacharach's work has had a profound impact on popular music. His collaborations with lyricist Hal David produced timeless classics like *Walk on By, What the World Needs Now Is Love, Raindrops Keep Fallin' on My Head*, and *I Say a Little Prayer*. Bacharach's music, characterized by its elegance, emotional depth, and musical complexity, offers invaluable lessons for songwriters looking to elevate their craft.

One of the most significant lessons from Burt Bacharach is the **importance of melody**. Bacharach was a master of crafting unforgettable, emotionally resonant melodies that feel both effortless and deeply expressive. His songs often featured long, sweeping melodic lines that avoided the typical repetition of pop music, giving them a more sophisticated and unpredictable quality. In *Alfie*, for example, the melody soars and dips in unexpected ways, perfectly capturing the introspective and philosophical nature of the lyrics.

For songwriters, this highlights the value of **creating melodies that stand out**. Rather than relying on simple, repetitive hooks, consider exploring more dynamic and fluid melodic structures that evolve over the course of the song. Bacharach's melodies often had a conversational quality, as if the music were telling a story, making them emotionally engaging and memorable. Experiment with longer phrases and varied melodic contours to create melodies that feel fresh and emotionally nuanced.

Another key lesson from Bacharach is his **innovative use of harmony**. Bacharach was known for incorporating complex, jazz-influenced chord progressions into his pop songs, often using unexpected modulations, key changes, and dissonant chords to create tension and release. In songs like *The Look of Love* and *I Say a Little Prayer*, he employed lush harmonies that gave the music a sense of sophistication and depth. His use of unusual chord voicings and progressions added layers of emotional complexity to even the simplest lyrics.

For songwriters, this shows the power of **experimenting with harmony** to enhance the emotional impact of a song. Rather than sticking to predictable chord progressions, explore more adventurous harmonic choices—such as using suspended chords, major sevenths, or diminished chords—to add emotional richness and depth. Bacharach's harmonies often created a sense of longing or tension that resolved beautifully, making the emotional journey of the song feel more satisfying. By thinking more creatively about harmony, you can add subtle layers of emotion to your music.

BACHARACH'S SONGS ALSO demonstrate the **importance of dynamics and musical texture**. His arrangements were often intricate, with carefully chosen instrumentation that enhanced the emotional tone of the song. Bacharach's background in orchestration and conducting allowed him to create rich musical landscapes, blending strings, brass, woodwinds, and rhythm sections to build dynamic, emotionally resonant pieces. In *Raindrops Keep Fallin' on My Head*, for instance, the light, bouncy rhythm and playful horn section create a sense of optimism and resilience that complements the song's lyrical message.

For songwriters, this highlights the value of **using instrumentation and arrangement to support the emotional narrative** of a song. Even in simple acoustic or piano-based songs, the choice of how instruments are layered and how dynamics shift throughout the song can profoundly affect its emotional impact. Bacharach's use of lush, intricate arrangements serves as a reminder to think beyond just melody and lyrics—consider how the texture and instrumentation of your song can enhance the overall mood and emotional arc.

Bacharach's music often **defied traditional pop structures**, embracing a more fluid, unpredictable approach to songwriting. While many pop songs adhere to a standard verse-chorus-verse structure, Bacharach often employed more complex forms that allowed the music to evolve organically. His songs frequently featured key changes, bridges that took unexpected harmonic turns, and choruses that felt like natural extensions of the verses rather than distinct, repetitive sections. In *This Guy's in Love with You*, for example, the song's structure flows seamlessly, with the melody and chords constantly shifting, creating a sense of emotional progression rather than repetition.

For songwriters, this shows the importance of **breaking away from formulaic structures** to create songs that feel more natural and emotionally authentic. While traditional song structures can be effective, experimenting with form can lead to more interesting and unique songs. Bacharach's music often felt like it was unfolding in real-time, with the structure serving the emotional journey of the song rather than adhering to predictable patterns. Try playing with different song structures, and don't be afraid to let the music take unexpected turns if it enhances the story or emotion.

Another key lesson from Burt Bacharach's songwriting is his ability to **pair complex music with simple, relatable lyrics**. His collaborations with Hal David produced some of the most emotionally direct and relatable lyrics in pop music, often dealing with themes like love, heartbreak, and yearning. In songs like *Walk on By* and *What the World Needs Now Is Love*, the lyrics are straightforward and universal, while the music provides emotional depth and sophistication. This contrast between the simplicity of the lyrics and the complexity of the music creates a balanced, emotionally resonant experience.

For songwriters, this emphasizes the importance of **balancing complexity and simplicity** in your work. While it's tempting to make everything in a song complex—whether it's the melody, harmony, or lyrics—Bacharach's music shows that sometimes the most powerful songs are those that combine simple, heartfelt lyrics with more intricate musical elements. The emotional clarity of the lyrics allows listeners to connect with the song on a personal level, while the sophistication of the music adds depth and richness.

Bacharach's ability to **write timeless songs** that feel both contemporary and classic is another invaluable lesson. His songs have endured for decades because they tap into universal emotions and are written with a sense of craftsmanship that transcends trends. *I Say a Little Prayer* or *The Look of Love* still feel relevant today because the emotions they express are timeless, and the melodies and harmonies are so well-crafted that they remain fresh to new generations of listeners.

For songwriters, this highlights the importance of **focusing on timeless emotions and themes**. While it's easy to get caught up in writing music that reflects current trends, songs that last are often those that speak to universal human experiences—love, loss, hope, and connection. By focusing on emotions that resonate across time and generations, and by crafting melodies and harmonies that feel well-constructed and original, you can create songs that have staying power.

One of the most remarkable aspects of Bacharach's songwriting is his **attention to detail**. His songs are meticulously crafted, with every note, chord, and rhythmic element carefully considered to serve the emotional and musical narrative. Bacharach was known for taking his time with songwriting, often refining melodies and harmonies until they were just right. This level of craftsmanship is part of what makes his songs feel so polished and emotionally effective.

For songwriters, this is a reminder of the value of **patience and precision** in songwriting. While inspiration often strikes quickly, great songs often require time and careful attention to detail to reach their full potential. Bacharach's songs are a testament to the importance of taking the time to refine and perfect your work, ensuring that every element of the song contributes to its emotional and musical impact.

Finally, Bacharach's **collaborative approach** to songwriting offers an important lesson for songwriters. His long-standing partnership with Hal David was built on a deep understanding of each other's strengths, with David's lyrics providing the perfect complement to Bacharach's melodies. This collaboration allowed them to create songs that were both lyrically and musically compelling, and their ability to work together so seamlessly was a key factor in their success.

For songwriters, this demonstrates the value of **collaboration** in the creative process. Working with other songwriters, musicians, or producers can bring fresh perspectives and ideas to your music, pushing you to explore new directions and refine your work. By finding collaborators who complement your strengths, you can create songs that are richer and more dynamic than you might have been able to achieve on your own.

In conclusion, Burt Bacharach's songwriting offers invaluable lessons in melody, harmony, and emotional expression. From his sophisticated use of harmony and dynamics to his ability to pair complex music with simple, relatable lyrics, Bacharach's work demonstrates the importance of craftsmanship and emotional authenticity in songwriting. His attention to detail, willingness to break from conventional structures, and focus on timeless emotions have made his music enduring and impactful. For songwriters, the lessons from Bacharach's work can help elevate your songwriting, allowing you to create songs that are both musically sophisticated and emotionally resonant.

Lessons from John Denver: Connecting with Nature and Authenticity in Songwriting

<hr>

John Denver, known for his gentle folk melodies and heartfelt lyrics, became one of the most beloved and influential songwriters of the 1970s. His music is characterized by its deep connection to nature, simplicity, and emotional authenticity. Denver's songs, such as *Take Me Home, Country Roads, Rocky Mountain High*, and *Annie's Song*, reflect his love for the natural world and his ability to communicate universal emotions with sincerity and clarity. For songwriters, Denver's work provides valuable lessons on how to connect with listeners by drawing on personal experiences, using vivid imagery, and writing from a place of genuine emotional truth.

One of the most important lessons from John Denver is the power of **writing from personal experience**. Denver's music was often inspired by his own life—his love of nature, his relationships, and his desire for simplicity and peace. Songs like *Rocky Mountain High* and *Take Me Home, Country Roads* reflect Denver's deep connection to the places he loved, particularly the natural landscapes of West Virginia and Colorado. The personal nature of these songs made them more relatable, as listeners could feel the authenticity and emotional depth behind the lyrics.

For songwriters, this demonstrates the importance of **writing from your own experiences and emotions**. When you write from a place of personal truth, your songs become more genuine and relatable. Denver's ability to capture the beauty of his surroundings and express his love for nature and home was part of what made his music so enduring. When crafting your own songs, consider drawing inspiration from the places, people, and moments that mean the most to you. By tapping into your personal experiences, you can create songs that resonate with listeners on a deeper level.

Another key lesson from John Denver's songwriting is his use of **nature and imagery** to evoke powerful emotions. Denver often used vivid imagery of the natural world to convey deeper emotional truths. In *Rocky Mountain High*, for example, Denver sings about the beauty and majesty of the Rocky Mountains as a metaphor for his own personal growth and spiritual awakening. The lyrics—"He was born in the summer of his 27th year / Coming home to a place he'd never been before"—use the natural landscape as a way to express feelings of freedom, discovery, and inner peace.

For songwriters, this highlights the value of **using imagery to convey emotions**. Nature, in particular, can be a powerful tool for evoking feelings of serenity, wonder, or nostalgia. By using sensory details—what the listener can see, hear, feel, and even smell—you can transport them into the world of your song and create a more immersive emotional experience. Denver's use of nature as a backdrop for his songs gives them a sense of timelessness and universality, allowing listeners to connect with the music on both a personal and emotional level.

<hr>

DENVER WAS ALSO KNOWN for his **simple, yet deeply emotional melodies**. Many of his most famous songs feature straightforward chord progressions and singable melodies that are easy to remember, but it's the sincerity of his performance and the emotional depth of the lyrics that give them their power. In *Annie's Song*, for example, Denver uses a simple, flowing melody to express his overwhelming love and devotion to his then-wife. The song's melody mirrors the natural beauty of the emotions he's expressing, creating a sense of harmony between the music and the lyrics.

For songwriters, this demonstrates the importance of **simplicity in melody**. A strong, memorable melody doesn't have to be complex—it just needs to feel authentic and emotionally true. Denver's melodies are often easy to sing and accessible to a wide audience, but they carry a deep emotional resonance because they are honest and heartfelt. When crafting your own melodies, focus on creating something that complements the emotional tone of the lyrics. Sometimes, the simplest melodies are the ones that resonate the most.

Another key aspect of John Denver's songwriting is his focus on **universal themes**. His songs often explore themes of love, home, nature, and the search for meaning—all of which are emotions and experiences that listeners can relate to. In *Take Me Home, Country Roads*, Denver sings about the longing for home, a feeling that resonates with people from all walks of life. The song's chorus—"Country roads, take me home / To the place I belong"—is both personal and universal, capturing the deep emotional connection people feel to their roots and their sense of belonging.

For songwriters, this underscores the importance of **writing about universal emotions**. Even when drawing on personal experiences, it's important to tap into feelings that listeners can relate to—love, loss, joy, longing, and connection. Denver's ability to write about these emotions in a way that felt genuine and personal, while still resonating with a wide audience, is part of what made his songs so impactful. When writing your own lyrics, consider how your personal experiences reflect broader emotional truths, and find ways to express those feelings in a way that speaks to the listener.

Denver's music is also a testament to the **power of positivity** in songwriting. While many songwriters explore darker or more melancholic themes, Denver's songs often express a sense of optimism, hope, and gratitude. In *Sunshine on My Shoulders*, for example, Denver reflects on the simple joy of feeling the sun's warmth, turning a small, everyday moment into something profound. His songs often celebrate the beauty of life, nature, and human connection, offering listeners a sense of peace and upliftment.

For songwriters, this shows the value of **writing songs that celebrate joy and positivity**. While it's important to explore a wide range of emotions in songwriting, Denver's work reminds us that music can also be a source of comfort, inspiration, and positivity. Writing songs that focus on gratitude, beauty, or hope can have a powerful impact on listeners, especially during times of difficulty or uncertainty. Denver's music often provided solace and inspiration for his listeners, which is one of the reasons his songs continue to be beloved today.

Another lesson from John Denver is his **emphasis on storytelling** in songwriting. Many of his songs tell simple, heartfelt stories about love, life, and the human experience. In *Back Home Again*, for example, Denver tells the story of returning home after being away, capturing the joy of reuniting with loved ones. The lyrics are straightforward but filled with warmth and sincerity, allowing listeners to feel the emotion behind the story.

For songwriters, this demonstrates the power of **storytelling to convey emotion**. Even if the story you're telling is a simple one, the way you tell it can have a profound emotional impact. Denver's ability to craft songs that felt like personal stories helped create a sense of intimacy and connection with his audience. When writing your own songs, think about how you can use storytelling to bring the listener into the world of the song and help them connect with the emotions behind it.

Finally, John Denver's music teaches the importance of **authenticity and sincerity** in songwriting. His songs were never overly complicated or pretentious—they were simple, honest reflections of his life, his love for nature, and his deep emotional connections to the people and places he cared about. This authenticity is what made his music so relatable and enduring. Denver didn't try to be something he wasn't; instead, he embraced his genuine love for folk music and the outdoors, and that sincerity came through in every song he wrote.

For songwriters, this is perhaps the most valuable lesson of all: **be true to yourself**. Write from the heart, and don't try to fit into trends or write what you think people want to hear. The most powerful songs are those that come from a place of honesty and vulnerability, where the songwriter expresses their true emotions and experiences. Denver's music reminds us that when we write from a place of authenticity, we create songs that resonate with listeners on a deep, emotional level.

In conclusion, John Denver's songwriting offers invaluable lessons in how to connect with listeners through simplicity, authenticity, and emotional truth. From his use of nature and imagery to evoke powerful emotions, to his focus on universal themes and positive storytelling, Denver's work demonstrates the power of heartfelt, genuine songwriting. By writing from personal experience, crafting memorable melodies, and telling simple yet profound stories, songwriters can learn to create music that speaks to the heart and endures for generations, just as Denver's songs continue to do today.

Writing Songs That Resonate with Listeners

Writing songs that resonate with listeners is one of the most important goals for any songwriter. A song that truly connects with an audience can evoke strong emotions, inspire memories, or offer comfort during difficult times. Whether through relatable lyrics, captivating melodies, or the emotional authenticity of the performance, a great song has the power to reach deep into the listener's heart. To achieve this, songwriters must craft music that speaks to universal emotions, tells meaningful stories, and conveys sincerity. Let's explore some key strategies for writing songs that resonate with listeners.

One of the most essential elements of a resonant song is the **emotional authenticity** behind it. Listeners can tell when a song is coming from a place of genuine feeling, and this authenticity makes the song more powerful. Whether you're writing about love, loss, hope, or heartbreak, it's important to write from a place of personal truth. Even if the song's narrative isn't autobiographical, the emotions behind it should feel real. Authenticity is what allows listeners to connect with the song on a deeper level, as they can relate to the raw emotions being expressed.

For songwriters, this means tapping into your own experiences and emotions when writing. Don't be afraid to express vulnerability, whether it's through sadness, joy, anger, or confusion. Some of the most beloved songs come from artists who are willing to open up emotionally, such as Adele's *Someone Like You* or John Lennon's *Imagine*. These songs resonate because they feel honest, and listeners can see themselves reflected in the emotional journey of the lyrics. By being true to your feelings and experiences, you create a song that listeners will find meaningful and authentic.

Another important aspect of writing songs that resonate is **telling relatable stories**. Songs that tell a story—whether it's about personal experiences, relationships, or broader themes—often capture listeners' attention because they feel like journeys or narratives they can follow. A great story within a song can make it feel more engaging and immersive, pulling the listener into the world you're creating. This doesn't mean the story has to be complicated—it can be simple, but if it's told with emotional depth and care, it will resonate.

For example, Bruce Springsteen's *The River* tells the story of a young couple facing the struggles of life in a small town. While the details of the story are specific to the characters in the song, the themes of love, hardship, and dreams deferred are universal, allowing listeners to connect with the song on an emotional level. Similarly, Dolly Parton's *Jolene* tells a simple yet powerful story of love and jealousy, and its emotional directness is what makes it so impactful. When writing your own songs, consider how you can use storytelling to engage listeners emotionally and take them on a journey.

Universal themes are another crucial element in songs that resonate with listeners. While every songwriter's experiences are unique, the emotions behind those experiences are often universal—love, heartbreak, longing, joy, and fear are emotions we all experience. Songs that focus on these universal themes tend to have broader appeal because listeners can easily relate to the emotions being expressed. For example, a love song about heartbreak will resonate with anyone who has experienced unrequited love or a difficult breakup, even if the details of the story differ from their own.

To write songs that resonate with a wide audience, focus on the **core emotions** behind the story or experience you're writing about. Even if the specific circumstances of your song are personal, consider how the underlying emotions—whether it's love, fear, hope, or sorrow—can be made relatable to a broader audience. Songs like Bob Dylan's *Blowin' in the Wind* or Leonard Cohen's *Hallelujah* resonate not because they tell a specific, personal story, but because they tap into universal human emotions and questions. When crafting your lyrics, think about how you can explore these shared experiences in a way that feels both personal and accessible.

Simplicity is another key factor in songs that resonate with listeners. While complex lyrics and melodies can be impressive, it's often the simplest songs that make the biggest emotional impact. A straightforward, heartfelt lyric or a simple, memorable melody can stick with a listener long after the song is over. Simplicity allows the core emotion of the song to shine through without distraction, making it easier for listeners to connect with the message. For example, Simon & Garfunkel's *The Sound of Silence* features simple, poetic lyrics and a haunting melody that convey a deep sense of loneliness and longing.

For songwriters, this doesn't mean you have to avoid complexity altogether, but it's important to ensure that the **emotional clarity of the song isn't lost** in complicated arrangements or overly ornate lyrics. Simple melodies and lyrics often have the greatest potential to resonate because they are easy to follow and emotionally direct. When writing a song, ask yourself: What is the central emotion or message I want to convey? Then, make sure that everything in the song—melody, harmony, lyrics—serves that emotional goal. Simplicity can be a powerful tool for ensuring that your song resonates with listeners on a deeper level.

In addition to simplicity, **memorable melodies** play a crucial role in making a song resonate. A great melody sticks with the listener long after they've heard the song, creating a sense of emotional attachment. Melodies that are singable and easy to remember often have the most lasting impact. Think of songs like The Beatles' *Yesterday* or Billie Eilish's *When the Party's Over*—both feature simple, haunting melodies that immediately capture the listener's attention and stay with them. A strong melody enhances the emotional message of the lyrics and makes the song more engaging and impactful.

To create memorable melodies, experiment with **repetition and variation**. Repeating a melody throughout a song helps establish it in the listener's mind, but adding subtle variations—such as changing the melody slightly in the chorus or bridge—can keep it fresh and interesting. Finding the balance between familiarity and surprise is key to crafting a melody that resonates emotionally. When paired with emotionally honest lyrics, a memorable melody can elevate the song to a new level, making it more likely to resonate with listeners.

DYNAMICS AND CONTRAST also play an important role in creating songs that resonate. A song that moves through different emotional or musical dynamics—such as shifting from soft, introspective verses to loud, powerful choruses—can take the listener on a more engaging emotional journey. This dynamic contrast mirrors the ebb and flow of emotions, making the song feel more alive and relatable. For example, in *Smells Like Teen Spirit* by Nirvana, the quiet verses and explosive choruses create a powerful sense of tension and release, amplifying the raw emotions behind the song.

For songwriters, this means considering how you can use **dynamics and contrast** to enhance the emotional arc of the song. Building intensity through the arrangement or performance can heighten the emotional impact, making the song more compelling for listeners. By changing the volume, tempo, or energy level of different sections of the song, you can create a more engaging and resonant experience.

Lastly, writing songs that resonate with listeners often comes down to **trusting your instincts** as a songwriter. While it's helpful to learn from the techniques of other successful songwriters, the most important thing is to stay true to your own voice and emotions. Listeners respond to songs that feel genuine, so it's crucial to write from a place of honesty and personal connection. Whether you're expressing joy, pain, love, or fear, let your own experiences guide the songwriting process, and don't be afraid to take creative risks in the pursuit of emotional truth.

In conclusion, writing songs that resonate with listeners requires a combination of emotional authenticity, relatable themes, memorable melodies, and thoughtful dynamics. By focusing on universal emotions, using simple yet powerful melodies, and telling stories that engage the listener, you can create songs that leave a lasting impact. Whether drawing on personal experiences or crafting broader narratives, the key is to write from the heart and stay true to your unique voice. When you do that, your songs will have the potential to connect deeply with listeners and resonate for years to come.

Experimenting with Unconventional Song Structures

One of the most exciting ways to push the boundaries of your songwriting and keep your music fresh is by experimenting with unconventional song structures. While traditional structures such as verse-chorus-verse or verse-chorus-bridge are common and effective, breaking away from these predictable forms can lead to more dynamic, engaging, and innovative songs. Songwriters who challenge traditional song structures often create music that surprises and captivates listeners by playing with form, structure, and flow in unexpected ways. Let's explore why experimenting with unconventional structures can elevate your songwriting and how you can effectively incorporate these approaches into your own music.

First, it's important to understand why **traditional song structures** are so commonly used in pop, rock, and many other genres. Structures like verse-chorus-verse-chorus-bridge-chorus create a sense of familiarity and predictability for listeners. The verse introduces the story or idea, the chorus delivers the emotional or thematic core of the song, and the bridge provides contrast or development before returning to the chorus. This repetition makes the song easy to follow and remember, which is why it works so well in mainstream music. However, while traditional structures are effective, they can sometimes limit creativity or lead to songs that feel formulaic.

By experimenting with unconventional structures, you can **break free from predictable patterns** and create songs that feel more unique, exploratory, or emotionally complex. Unconventional structures might involve shifting between different sections without repeating a chorus, avoiding a typical verse-chorus structure, or introducing sections that are unexpected or asymmetrical. For instance, you could write a song that uses only verses with no chorus at all, or one that starts with a bridge and then moves into verses. These structural choices can make your music feel less predictable and more engaging because listeners won't immediately know where the song is going.

One of the most famous examples of an unconventional structure is Queen's *Bohemian Rhapsody*. The song abandons the verse-chorus format in favor of a multi-section composition that moves through various musical styles and emotions without returning to any single motif. The song begins with a ballad-like introduction, shifts into an operatic section, and ends with a hard rock finale, creating an epic journey. Despite its unconventional form, *Bohemian Rhapsody* became a huge success, showing that listeners can appreciate complex and surprising structures when they are executed well.

For songwriters, this highlights the importance of **embracing structural fluidity**. You don't have to be bound by the expectation of repetition or return to familiar sections. Consider how your song might evolve naturally, and let the structure reflect that progression rather than adhering to a preset formula. For example, if your song starts with a soft, introspective melody, you could build it gradually toward a climactic section, avoiding the typical "return to the chorus" pattern. This approach can create a more immersive emotional experience, allowing the song to unfold organically rather than predictably.

NON-REPEATING STRUCTURES are another unconventional approach worth exploring. Songs like The Beatles' *A Day in the Life* or Radiohead's *Paranoid Android* have structures that feel more like a journey or progression than a repetition of verses and choruses. These songs move through different musical ideas without returning to earlier sections, creating a sense of forward motion. The lack of repetition keeps the listener engaged, as each section introduces something new. This type of structure works particularly well for songs that tell a story or explore different emotional states, as the music can evolve alongside the narrative.

If you want to experiment with non-repeating structures, think about how you can use **contrast and variation** to keep the song interesting. Without the anchor of a repeating chorus, you'll need to create interest by introducing new musical ideas, dynamic changes, or shifts in tempo or key. Each section of the song should feel distinct yet connected, taking the listener on a journey through different moods or themes. This approach can result in songs that feel more like cinematic or emotional experiences than traditional pop songs.

Another technique for breaking away from conventional structures is to experiment with **asymmetrical forms**. Traditional song structures are often built on symmetrical patterns—four bars of verse, four bars of chorus, etc.—but asymmetrical forms can create a sense of unpredictability and tension. For example, you might write a song where the verses are six bars long while the chorus is only three bars, or where different sections have varying lengths. This imbalance can create a more dynamic and interesting listening experience, as the structure feels less predictable and more fluid.

In songs like Pink Floyd's *Money*, asymmetrical time signatures and uneven phrase lengths add to the song's unique feel. *Money* is in 7/4 time, which gives it an unusual rhythmic structure compared to typical 4/4 pop songs. The asymmetry in the rhythm and phrasing keeps the listener on their toes and makes the song feel distinctive. For songwriters, experimenting with **unusual time signatures** or irregular phrasing can create a similar effect, giving your music a sense of uniqueness and tension that might not be achievable with more conventional structures.

Layering multiple musical ideas within a single song can also create a more complex structure. Instead of sticking to a single musical theme throughout the song, you could introduce contrasting sections that evolve and build on each other. David Bowie's *Space Oddity*, for instance, blends a folk-inspired intro with a more driving rock section in the middle, and then returns to the calm, spaced-out feel of the intro. The layering of different musical ideas creates a sense of narrative progression and adds depth to the song's emotional arc.

When experimenting with layering, think about how you can introduce **different musical or thematic elements** throughout the song. For example, you might start with a soft acoustic section and then build into a more electronic or rock-oriented section, creating contrast and interest. These transitions don't have to be jarring—they can be subtle and smooth, creating a sense of evolution rather than abrupt shifts. The key is to think about how each new section builds on or contrasts with what came before, creating a song that feels dynamic and multi-dimensional.

Another unconventional structure to explore is the **reverse structure**, where the song starts with what would traditionally be the climax or chorus and then works backward. This can create an interesting emotional arc, as the listener experiences the peak of the song's intensity right from the start and then follows the journey back to its origins. Songs like Radiohead's *Exit Music (For a Film)* build intensity early on and then strip back to more subdued sections, creating a powerful emotional experience that defies traditional expectations.

For songwriters, experimenting with **reverse dynamics** or starting with the song's most powerful section can create a unique sense of drama and tension. By flipping the typical progression of a song, you can surprise the listener and create a more unpredictable emotional journey. Think about how you can structure your song in a way that builds intensity in unconventional ways, whether it's by starting with the climax or gradually deconstructing the song as it progresses.

In conclusion, experimenting with unconventional song structures can open up new creative possibilities and help you craft songs that feel fresh, engaging, and emotionally impactful. Whether you're playing with non-repeating forms, asymmetrical phrasing, layered sections, or reverse structures, the key is to think about how the structure of the song can enhance the emotional narrative. By breaking away from traditional verse-chorus patterns, you can create music that surprises and captivates listeners, taking them on a journey that feels unique and deeply resonant.

Collaborating with Other Songwriters: Enhancing Creativity and Expanding Your Musical Horizons

Collaborating with other songwriters can be one of the most rewarding and transformative experiences for any musician. Working with others not only brings fresh perspectives and ideas to your music but also challenges you to step outside your comfort zone and explore new creative directions. Some of the most iconic songs and albums have come from successful collaborations between songwriters, blending their unique talents into something greater than the sum of its parts. From Lennon and McCartney to Elton John and Bernie Taupin, collaboration has been at the heart of many of the greatest works in music history. Let's explore the benefits of songwriting collaboration, strategies for making the most of it, and how to build a productive creative partnership.

One of the primary benefits of collaborating with other songwriters is that it **brings fresh ideas and perspectives** to your creative process. When you work alone, it's easy to fall into familiar patterns or habits, but collaborating forces you to think outside the box and approach songwriting from a different angle. Every songwriter has their own unique way of thinking about melody, lyrics, harmony, and structure, and when you bring these perspectives together, you create opportunities for creative breakthroughs that might not have been possible working solo.

For example, if you tend to focus on melody and harmony but struggle with lyrics, collaborating with a lyricist can open up new possibilities for how your music and lyrics interact. Conversely, if you're more of a wordsmith but struggle with writing catchy melodies, working with someone who excels in that area can elevate your songs. By combining your strengths with those of another songwriter, you can create music that feels more complete and well-rounded.

Collaboration also helps you **expand your musical horizons** by exposing you to different styles, genres, and approaches to songwriting. When you collaborate with someone who has a different musical background or set of influences, you're more likely to incorporate elements into your music that you wouldn't have thought of on your own. This kind of cross-pollination can lead to exciting musical results, as you blend your unique styles into something new.

Consider how artists like David Bowie and Brian Eno, or Paul Simon's collaboration with South African musicians on *Graceland*, pushed each other into new musical territories by bringing different influences and perspectives to the table. When you collaborate with someone who thinks differently or has a different musical toolkit, you're more likely to break new ground and create music that's innovative and exciting.

Another significant benefit of collaboration is the **shared creative energy** that comes from working with others. Songwriting can sometimes feel like a solitary process, but collaborating allows you to feed off the energy and enthusiasm of your co-writer(s). This energy can help spark creativity, making the process feel more dynamic and fluid. When ideas bounce back and forth between collaborators, the song often develops in unexpected and exciting ways, leading to a sense of momentum that can push the project forward more quickly than if you were working alone.

For songwriters, this dynamic exchange can be especially helpful during moments of creative block. If you're stuck on a song or struggling to come up with new ideas, working with someone else can reignite your creativity and help you see the song from a different perspective. A co-writer might suggest a chord change, lyric, or structural shift that takes the song in a direction you hadn't considered, helping you get unstuck and keep moving forward.

That said, collaboration also requires **trust and open communication** to be successful. One of the most important aspects of any songwriting partnership is the ability to communicate openly and honestly about ideas, suggestions, and feedback. You need to be willing to share your creative vision while also being receptive to the ideas and input of your collaborator. This means letting go of some control and being open to changes that may push the song in a direction you hadn't initially imagined.

For songwriters who are used to working alone, this can be a challenge, but it's essential for a successful collaboration. When working with others, it's important to approach the process with **an open mind and a willingness to compromise**. Not every idea you or your collaborator comes up with will make it into the final song, but by being flexible and open to experimentation, you can create something that feels truly collaborative and greater than the sum of its parts.

Effective collaboration also involves **defining roles** early in the process. In some collaborations, songwriters take on specific roles—one might focus on melody and harmony while the other handles lyrics and structure. In other cases, the songwriting process might be more fluid, with both collaborators contributing to every aspect of the song. Either approach can work, but it's important to establish how you and your co-writer will work together early on so that expectations are clear.

For example, in the legendary partnership of Elton John and Bernie Taupin, Taupin primarily wrote lyrics while John focused on composing melodies. This division of labor allowed each to focus on their strengths while still working together to create cohesive songs. On the other hand, Lennon and McCartney often wrote together in a more fluid way, contributing to both the lyrics and music of their songs, which created a different kind of creative synergy. Whether you prefer a more defined or fluid approach to collaboration, establishing how you'll work together can help streamline the process and ensure a more productive partnership.

Collaboration can also be a valuable learning experience, as it gives you the chance to **observe and adopt new techniques** from your co-writer. You may pick up new ways to approach melody, chord progressions, lyric writing, or arrangement simply by watching how your collaborator works. This exposure to different methods can broaden your own songwriting skillset and introduce you to techniques you might not have discovered on your own.

For example, you might learn how to approach lyric writing from a different angle by watching how your collaborator creates vivid imagery or structures their verses. Similarly, you might pick up new ways to experiment with rhythm or harmony by observing how another songwriter uses unconventional chord voicings or time signatures. Every collaboration is an opportunity to grow as a songwriter, both through the creative exchange of ideas and by learning from the unique approaches of others.

It's also important to remember that collaboration doesn't have to happen in person. **Remote collaborations** are increasingly common, especially in the digital age, where songwriters can easily share ideas and demos through email, cloud storage, or collaboration platforms like Splice. This can be especially beneficial if you want to work with someone in a different geographic location or if your schedules don't align for in-person writing sessions. Remote collaboration allows you to take your time with ideas, exchange feedback at your own pace, and still create great music without being in the same room.

However, remote collaboration also requires clear communication and a structured workflow to ensure that ideas don't get lost or misinterpreted. It's helpful to establish clear **milestones** or **deadlines** for different parts of the songwriting process—such as sending lyric drafts, recording demos, or finalizing arrangements—so that both collaborators stay on track and contribute in a timely manner.

Lastly, one of the most rewarding aspects of collaboration is the opportunity to **build creative relationships** that last. Some songwriting partnerships develop into long-term collaborations that span multiple projects, while others may only come together for a single song. Regardless of the length of the partnership, the connections you build through collaboration can be invaluable, both creatively and professionally. These relationships can lead to new opportunities, as well as ongoing support and inspiration from fellow songwriters who understand your creative process.

In conclusion, collaborating with other songwriters can enhance your creativity, introduce fresh ideas, and expand your musical horizons. Whether you're blending different styles, learning new techniques, or pushing each other to explore unfamiliar territory, collaboration offers the chance to create music that feels innovative and emotionally resonant. By fostering open communication, trusting your collaborator's input, and embracing the dynamic energy of shared creativity, you can elevate your songwriting to new heights and develop lasting partnerships that enrich your artistic journey.

Creating Hooks That Keep Listeners Engaged

A hook is one of the most essential elements of a song—it's the part that grabs the listener's attention and keeps them coming back for more. Whether it's a catchy melody, a memorable lyric, or an irresistible rhythm, a strong hook can be the difference between a song that fades into the background and one that sticks in a listener's mind long after the music has stopped. Hooks are particularly important in popular music, where listeners often respond to songs that have a distinctive, repeatable element. Creating hooks that engage and captivate listeners requires a blend of creativity, simplicity, and emotional resonance. Let's explore the key strategies for crafting hooks that leave a lasting impact.

One of the most important aspects of a hook is its **melodic catchiness**. Melodies that are simple, memorable, and easy to sing along with tend to make the strongest hooks. A hook's melody should feel natural, flowing in a way that listeners can follow and remember after just one listen. Think of songs like Taylor Swift's *Shake It Off* or Pharrell Williams's *Happy*—both feature simple yet incredibly catchy melodies that make the songs instantly recognizable. These hooks aren't overly complicated, but they are extremely effective because they stick in the listener's mind.

For songwriters, this means focusing on **simplicity and repetition** in your hook melodies. Repetition helps reinforce the melody in the listener's memory, making it more likely to stick. A hook that repeats key melodic phrases or patterns becomes more familiar with each listen, giving the song a sense of comfort and predictability. However, balance is key—while repetition is important, slight variations can add interest and prevent the hook from becoming monotonous.

In addition to melody, **lyrical hooks** play a crucial role in engaging listeners. A great lyrical hook often distills the central message or emotion of the song into a concise, memorable phrase. This could be the chorus or even a standout line within the verse. Songs like Adele's *Rolling in the Deep* or Journey's *Don't Stop Believin'* are anchored by powerful lyrical hooks that encapsulate the song's emotional core in a few words. The simplicity and directness of the lyrics make them easy for listeners to remember and sing along with, increasing the song's impact.

For songwriters, crafting a strong lyrical hook involves **choosing words that are emotionally resonant** and easy to repeat. The lyrics in a hook should feel universal—something listeners can relate to on a personal level. The hook in Whitney Houston's *I Will Always Love You* is a perfect example of this. The lyrics express a simple yet profound sentiment that resonates with listeners from all walks of life, making the song an enduring classic. When writing your own hooks, think about how you can convey a powerful emotion or message in as few words as possible, while maintaining clarity and impact.

ANOTHER KEY ELEMENT of an engaging hook is its **rhythmic appeal**. Hooks with distinctive rhythmic patterns can make a song stand out and keep listeners engaged. A rhythmic hook doesn't have to be complex—it just needs to have a groove that catches the listener's attention. In songs like Michael Jackson's *Billie Jean* or Justin Timberlake's *Can't Stop the Feeling*, the rhythm of the hook is an integral part of what makes the song so captivating. The syncopation and groove create an infectious energy that pulls the listener in.

For songwriters, this highlights the importance of **playing with rhythm and groove** when developing a hook. Experiment with different rhythms, syncopation, or even pauses to create a hook that feels fresh and dynamic. The rhythm of the hook should enhance the overall energy of the song, making it feel more compelling and engaging. Whether it's a driving beat or a laid-back groove, the right rhythm can elevate a hook and give it a distinctive, memorable feel.

In some cases, a **harmonic or instrumental hook** can be just as powerful as a vocal hook. Instrumental hooks—such as a memorable guitar riff, bass line, or synth melody—can create a strong sense of identity for the song. For instance, the iconic guitar riff in Deep Purple's *Smoke on the Water* or the pulsing synth line in A-ha's *Take on Me* are instantly recognizable and serve as the driving force behind the song's catchiness. Even without lyrics, these hooks engage listeners by providing a musical motif that sticks in their heads.

For songwriters and producers, this underscores the value of **exploring instrumental ideas** that can serve as hooks. Sometimes, a well-placed instrumental motif can become the signature element of a song. Experiment with different instruments, tones, and melodic patterns to find a hook that stands out. Instrumental hooks can complement lyrical and melodic hooks or stand on their own, adding another layer of engagement for listeners.

Contrast within a hook can also make it more effective. A hook that contrasts with the surrounding sections of the song—whether in terms of melody, rhythm, dynamics, or harmony—creates a sense of surprise and makes the hook stand out. For example, in Outkast's *Hey Ya!*, the chorus hook is rhythmically and melodically distinct from the verses, creating a dynamic shift that immediately grabs attention. This contrast not only keeps the listener engaged but also reinforces the hook's emotional and musical impact.

To use contrast effectively in your hooks, think about how you can **change the energy, rhythm, or tone** when the hook comes in. Whether it's a sudden shift to a higher or lower register, a rhythmic variation, or a change in dynamics, contrast can help make your hook more memorable by making it feel like the high point of the song. Experiment with creating a sense of tension in the verse and releasing it in the hook, or vice versa, to give your song a more dynamic flow.

REPETITION AND VARIATION are crucial techniques for creating hooks that stick with listeners. While repetition helps reinforce the hook in the listener's memory, variation keeps it interesting and prevents it from becoming too predictable. Songs like Katy Perry's *Roar* or The Beatles' *Hey Jude* use repetition to great effect, but they also introduce subtle changes in melody, harmony, or dynamics as the song progresses. This combination of repetition and variation creates a sense of familiarity while keeping the listener engaged.

When crafting your hooks, consider how you can introduce **small variations** as the song develops. This could involve changing the melody slightly in the second chorus, adding harmonies, or altering the rhythm to create a new texture. These variations keep the hook fresh while maintaining the core elements that make it memorable.

Pacing and timing are also important factors in creating hooks that engage listeners. The placement of a hook within the song can influence how effectively it grabs attention. In many pop songs, the hook is introduced early—often within the first 30 seconds—to ensure that listeners are hooked from the start. However, delaying the hook or building up to it can create a sense of anticipation that makes the eventual payoff even more satisfying. Songs like Adele's *Rolling in the Deep* build tension in the verses, creating anticipation for the powerful hook that follows.

For songwriters, this means thinking carefully about the **timing and delivery** of the hook. If your hook is particularly strong, you might want to introduce it early to capture the listener's attention right away. Alternatively, you could build suspense by delaying the hook and creating a sense of anticipation, making the listener eager for the moment when the hook finally arrives.

Finally, **emotional resonance** is one of the most important elements of a successful hook. A great hook not only engages the listener's ear but also connects with them on an emotional level. Whether it's a joyful, triumphant hook that makes the listener feel uplifted, or a melancholic hook that taps into feelings of sadness or nostalgia, the most memorable hooks are those that evoke a strong emotional response. Songs like Fleetwood Mac's *Go Your Own Way* or Sam Smith's *Stay with Me* resonate because their hooks are not just catchy—they also carry deep emotional weight.

For songwriters, this means focusing on **emotional clarity** in your hooks. Think about the emotion you want to convey and how the melody, lyrics, and rhythm can work together to express that feeling. A hook that makes the listener feel something—whether it's happiness, sadness, excitement, or longing—is more likely to resonate and stay with them long after the song ends.

In conclusion, creating hooks that keep listeners engaged involves a combination of catchy melodies, memorable lyrics, rhythmic appeal, and emotional resonance. By focusing on simplicity, repetition, contrast, and emotional depth, you can craft hooks that not only grab attention but also leave a lasting impression. Whether you're writing a vocal hook, instrumental motif, or rhythmic groove, the goal is to create something that listeners will want to hear over and over again. With the right balance of creativity and craftsmanship, your hooks can become the defining element of your songs, making them both memorable and meaningful to your audience.

Using Repetition for Impact: Enhancing Songwriting through Reinforcement and Emotion

Repetition is a powerful tool in songwriting that can create emotional resonance, reinforce key themes, and make a song more memorable for listeners. Whether used in melodies, lyrics, or rhythm, repetition helps establish familiarity and provides structure within a song, making it easier for audiences to connect with the music. When used thoughtfully, repetition can also amplify emotional impact and turn simple ideas into unforgettable moments. However, like any tool, repetition must be balanced carefully—overuse can make a song feel monotonous, while underuse can make it difficult for a listener to grasp the core message. Let's explore how to use repetition effectively to create songs that are both engaging and emotionally resonant.

One of the most important roles of repetition is its ability to **anchor the listener in the song**. A repeated phrase, melody, or rhythm creates a sense of familiarity, which helps the listener feel more connected to the music. In pop and rock music, the chorus is often built around repetition because it delivers the main message of the song and is meant to be the most memorable part. For example, in Adele's *Someone Like You*, the repeated chorus "Never mind, I'll find someone like you" becomes the emotional heart of the song, reinforcing the theme of heartbreak and longing.

For songwriters, this means using repetition to **highlight the key emotional moments** in the song. By repeating a line or phrase at critical points—whether in the chorus or elsewhere—you give the listener something to latch onto, making the song more impactful. The goal is to ensure that the repeated sections encapsulate the core emotion or message of the song, helping to create a stronger emotional connection between the music and the audience.

Repetition is also an effective way to **create and build tension** in a song. Repeating a melodic or lyrical idea can create anticipation, especially if slight variations are introduced with each repetition. This technique allows you to build up emotional intensity before releasing it in a climactic moment. For example, in *Hey Jude* by The Beatles, the extended repetition of the "Na-na-na-na" refrain creates an escalating sense of communal joy, leading to a powerful emotional release as the song builds to its climax.

For songwriters, this demonstrates how repetition can be used to **gradually heighten emotions**. By repeating a phrase or section and subtly increasing the intensity—through dynamic shifts, added harmonies, or instrumental layers—you can create an emotional arc that draws the listener in. The repeated section becomes more impactful with each iteration, culminating in a sense of resolution when the tension is finally released. This technique works especially well in choruses, bridges, or outros where you want to create a lasting emotional effect.

IN ADDITION TO BUILDING tension, repetition can also be used to create **a sense of unity and cohesion** within a song. Repeated motifs—whether melodic, lyrical, or rhythmic—can help tie different sections of a song together, making it feel more cohesive and connected. This technique is particularly useful when a song features contrasting sections, such as a soft verse followed by a powerful chorus. By reintroducing familiar elements throughout the song, you give the listener a sense of continuity, even as the music shifts in dynamics or mood.

For example, in Beyoncé's *Single Ladies (Put a Ring on It)*, the rhythmic repetition of the "oh-oh-oh" phrase throughout the song acts as a unifying element that ties the verses, pre-chorus, and chorus together. The repetition provides a through-line that helps the song feel cohesive while maintaining its high-energy vibe. For songwriters, this highlights the importance of using repetition to **anchor the listener amidst changing musical landscapes**. Whether through a repeating lyrical phrase or a recurring rhythmic pattern, repetition can help create structure and flow in a song.

Another effective use of repetition is in **reinforcing key lyrical themes**. Repeating certain lines or phrases can emphasize the central message or emotional core of the song, making it resonate more deeply with listeners. In Bob Dylan's *Blowin' in the Wind*, the repeated line "The answer, my friend, is blowin' in the wind" serves as both a philosophical statement and an emotional refrain, reinforcing the song's theme of uncertainty and longing for answers. The repetition makes the message feel more impactful and memorable, ensuring that the listener leaves the song with the central idea firmly in mind.

For songwriters, this means using repetition strategically to **reinforce the core message or emotion** of the song. By repeating key lines or phrases that encapsulate the essence of the song, you can drive home the emotional impact and make the lyrics more memorable. However, it's important to ensure that the repeated lines are meaningful and add depth to the song—overusing repetition without purpose can make the song feel shallow or monotonous.

Repetition can also be used to **play with listener expectations** by creating a sense of predictability and then breaking away from it. When listeners hear a repeated pattern, they begin to anticipate what comes next. By subtly altering the repeated phrase—either through a change in melody, harmony, or rhythm—you can surprise the listener and create a more dynamic listening experience. This technique is particularly effective when you want to create a sense of emotional shift or evolution within the song.

For example, in Radiohead's *Creep*, the repeated use of the phrase "I'm a creep" is suddenly interrupted by a powerful, distorted guitar riff that breaks the song's established pattern, creating a jarring and impactful moment. This unexpected shift heightens the emotional intensity of the song, leaving a lasting impression on the listener. For songwriters, this shows the value of **playing with repetition and variation**—by introducing small changes to a repeated pattern, you can keep the listener engaged and create moments of emotional surprise.

Repetitive rhythm is another powerful tool for engaging listeners. Repeating rhythmic patterns, especially in the bassline or percussion, creates a groove that can make the song feel more infectious and energizing. Songs like Queen's *We Will Rock You* use a simple, repetitive rhythm to create a communal, anthemic feel. The repetition of the iconic stomps and claps not only makes the song instantly recognizable but also encourages audience participation, making the song feel more interactive and engaging.

For songwriters, this highlights the importance of **rhythmic repetition** in creating a memorable and engaging hook. Repeated rhythms help establish a groove that listeners can latch onto, making the song feel more immediate and inviting. Whether it's through drums, bass, or other percussive elements, rhythmic repetition can help drive the energy of the song and keep the listener engaged from start to finish.

Melodic repetition is equally effective, especially when used in combination with a strong lyric or rhythmic hook. Repeating a melody within the chorus, for example, helps cement the hook in the listener's mind, making it more likely that they will remember and sing along with the song. In Pharrell Williams's *Happy*, the repetitive, upbeat melody in the chorus reinforces the joyful mood of the song, making it feel infectious and irresistible.

For songwriters, this means focusing on creating **melodic phrases that are easy to repeat and sing along with**. A memorable melody that repeats throughout the song, especially in the chorus, makes the song more accessible to listeners and increases its chances of becoming a hit. When crafting a melody, think about how you can use repetition to make the tune more familiar without sacrificing its originality or emotional depth.

It's also important to note that **too much repetition** can lead to predictability, which can make a song feel monotonous or uninteresting. To avoid this, consider how you can balance repetition with variation. For example, you might repeat a phrase in the first two choruses but introduce a new element—such as a vocal harmony or instrumental counter-melody—during the final chorus to keep the listener engaged. By making small adjustments, you can prevent the song from becoming too repetitive while still maintaining the power of repeated elements.

In conclusion, using repetition for impact is about finding the right balance between familiarity and variation. Repetition helps create structure, reinforces key themes, and makes a song more memorable, but it needs to be used with purpose and creativity to avoid feeling monotonous. By using repetition strategically—whether in melody, lyrics, rhythm, or harmonic patterns—you can enhance the emotional resonance of your songs, create anticipation, and make your music more engaging and memorable for listeners. With the right approach, repetition can be one of the most effective tools in your songwriting arsenal, helping to create songs that stick with your audience long after the music has stopped.

The Importance of a Strong Chorus: Crafting the Emotional and Musical Heart of a Song

The chorus is the center-piece of most popular songs, serving as the emotional and musical anchor that ties the entire composition together. A strong chorus is often the part of the song that listeners remember most, the section they sing along to, and the moment when the song's core message or feeling is fully realized. While verses and bridges provide context and development, the chorus is where the song's energy and emotion typically reach their peak. Crafting a powerful chorus is essential for creating a song that resonates with listeners and leaves a lasting impression. Let's explore the elements that make a chorus strong and how songwriters can create choruses that elevate their music.

One of the key reasons a strong chorus is so important is that it **encapsulates the main theme or emotion** of the song. The chorus distills the song's central message or feeling into a concise, repeatable section that reinforces what the song is about. Whether it's a joyful anthem, a heart-wrenching ballad, or an empowering statement, the chorus is the space where the song's emotional core is crystallized. This is why choruses often feature the title of the song and summarize the key lyrical or emotional point the songwriter wants to make.

For songwriters, this means that the chorus should **clearly communicate the essence of the song**. Whether you're writing about love, loss, triumph, or reflection, the chorus should feel like the emotional high point where the listener connects with the song's message. In songs like Journey's *Don't Stop Believin'*, the chorus serves as both a lyrical and emotional summary, delivering a message of hope and perseverance. By focusing the chorus on the song's central theme, you give the listener a clear point of emotional connection.

A strong chorus also serves as the **melodic focal point** of the song. While the verses may introduce more complex or narrative-driven ideas, the chorus often features the most **memorable melody**—the part that sticks in the listener's mind. A catchy, singable melody is crucial for a successful chorus because it makes the song more accessible and easy to remember. Think of songs like Katy Perry's *Firework* or Queen's *We Are the Champions*—the chorus melody is the part that everyone knows, even after just one listen.

For songwriters, crafting a memorable melodic hook for the chorus is essential. The melody should be **simple, yet impactful**, and it should contrast with the verses in a way that elevates the emotional intensity. One effective approach is to use a melody in the chorus that is higher in pitch than the verses, creating a sense of lift and climax. This melodic contrast helps the chorus feel like the emotional and musical peak of the song, giving listeners something to latch onto. Repetition of the melody within the chorus also reinforces its memorability, making it more likely to stick with the listener.

ANOTHER IMPORTANT ELEMENT of a strong chorus is its **lyrical simplicity and directness**. While verses often explore more detailed or complex ideas, the chorus is usually the part of the song where the message is distilled into its simplest and most impactful form. This doesn't mean the lyrics have to be simplistic, but they should be **clear and easy to understand**. A chorus with too many words or overly complex phrasing can feel cluttered, making it harder for the listener to engage with the song. In contrast, a chorus that uses direct, relatable language is more likely to resonate with a broad audience.

For example, in Adele's *Rolling in the Deep*, the chorus lyrics—"We could have had it all"—are simple but loaded with emotional weight. The clarity of the message allows the listener to feel the full impact of the song's theme of lost love and betrayal. Similarly, in Bon Jovi's *Livin' on a Prayer*, the chorus is direct and anthemic, expressing resilience in the face of adversity. For songwriters, this demonstrates the importance of **keeping the chorus lyrics focused on the emotional core** of the song, using simple but powerful language to convey the message.

The **structure and rhythm** of a chorus are also crucial to its effectiveness. A strong chorus often contrasts with the verses in terms of rhythm, providing a clear shift in energy. In many cases, the chorus has a more driving, powerful rhythm than the verses, helping to elevate the song's intensity and create a sense of climax. This rhythmic change can make the chorus feel like a release of built-up tension, giving the listener a sense of satisfaction when it finally arrives.

For example, in Beyoncé's *Single Ladies (Put a Ring on It)*, the verses are more rhythmically syncopated, but when the chorus hits, the rhythm becomes more driving and straightforward, making the hook more impactful. This shift in rhythm helps to make the chorus stand out and feel like the high point of the song. For songwriters, experimenting with **rhythmic contrast between verses and chorus** can create a more dynamic listening experience, ensuring that the chorus feels like a rewarding payoff after the verse.

Repetition is another critical factor in creating a strong chorus. Repeating key phrases, both lyrically and melodically, within the chorus helps reinforce the message and makes the song more memorable. This repetition creates familiarity, which makes the song easier to remember and sing along with. In songs like Rihanna's *Umbrella* or The Beatles' *Hey Jude*, the chorus uses repetition to great effect, making the song instantly recognizable and easy for listeners to engage with.

For songwriters, repetition is a powerful tool, but it must be used **with care**. Over-repetition can lead to a chorus feeling repetitive or monotonous, so it's important to strike a balance. One effective strategy is to introduce **slight variations** in the melody or lyrics with each repetition of the chorus. This keeps the repetition interesting while still providing the listener with the familiar hook that makes the chorus memorable. Adding layers, such as vocal harmonies or instrumental changes, during each repeat of the chorus can also help maintain the listener's interest.

CONTRAST BETWEEN THE verse and the chorus is another key element of a strong chorus. A chorus that contrasts with the verse in terms of melody, harmony, rhythm, or dynamics creates a clear distinction between the two sections, making the chorus feel more impactful when it arrives. This contrast helps to build anticipation, as the listener feels a natural pull toward the more intense or climactic section of the song. For example, in Coldplay's *Fix You*, the soft, delicate verses contrast with the soaring, anthemic chorus, creating a powerful emotional shift when the chorus hits.

For songwriters, creating **contrast between the verse and chorus** can be achieved in several ways. You might use a different chord progression in the chorus that feels more uplifting or dramatic, or you could shift from a quieter dynamic in the verse to a louder, more energetic chorus. By making the chorus feel like a distinct and elevated section, you ensure that it stands out and delivers the emotional punch that keeps listeners engaged.

A strong chorus also provides **emotional release** for the listener. After the build-up and tension of the verses, the chorus offers a sense of resolution or catharsis, where the emotions of the song are fully expressed. This emotional release is what makes choruses so satisfying—listeners are drawn to the part of the song where the tension is resolved, and the core message is delivered with full intensity. In songs like Whitney Houston's *I Will Always Love You*, the chorus is where the song's deepest emotions are laid bare, creating a moment of pure emotional release for both the singer and the listener.

For songwriters, thinking about how the chorus can provide **emotional resolution** or climax is essential. Whether the song is joyful, sorrowful, or empowering, the chorus should feel like the moment when the emotion reaches its peak. This is where the listener experiences the full weight of the song's message, so it's important to ensure that the melody, lyrics, and dynamics work together to deliver that emotional impact.

In conclusion, a strong chorus is the heart of a song, providing both musical and emotional structure. It serves as the moment where the song's message is crystallized, offering listeners a clear and memorable point of connection. By focusing on crafting a memorable melody, keeping the lyrics simple and direct, using repetition and contrast, and building toward an emotional climax, songwriters can create choruses that not only engage listeners but also stay with them long after the song is over. A well-crafted chorus elevates the entire song, making it more impactful, memorable, and resonant for the audience.

Writing Verses That Build a Narrative: Crafting a Story through Song

While the chorus often serves as the emotional or thematic core of a song, the verses are where the story unfolds. Writing verses that build a narrative is an essential part of songwriting, especially for songs that seek to engage the listener on a deeper, more emotional level. Verses are the foundation of the song's narrative structure, providing the context, details, and progression that lead to the chorus. Whether you're telling a literal story or exploring a more abstract emotional journey, the verses allow you to develop characters, build tension, and set the stage for the chorus's resolution. Let's explore how to write verses that build a compelling narrative, keeping listeners engaged from start to finish.

One of the most important aspects of writing verses that build a narrative is **establishing a clear setting or context** in the opening verse. This gives the listener a sense of where the song is taking place—whether it's a physical location, an emotional state, or a specific situation. By grounding the listener in a setting, you create a framework for the story or message to unfold. For example, in Bruce Springsteen's *The River*, the first verse immediately sets the scene by introducing the characters, their relationship, and the economic struggles they face: "I come from down in the valley / Where, mister, when you're young / They bring you up to do like your daddy done."

For songwriters, this means **using the first verse to establish the "who," "where," and "what"** of the song. Whether you're telling a straightforward story or exploring an emotional landscape, the first verse should provide enough information to hook the listener and make them want to know more. This doesn't mean you have to reveal everything at once—sometimes hinting at details can create intrigue—but setting up a clear sense of context helps the listener follow the narrative as it unfolds.

Once the setting and context are established, the verses should **move the narrative forward** by introducing new details, emotions, or perspectives. Each verse should build on the previous one, adding layers of meaning or complexity to the story. In storytelling, this is known as the rising action—the gradual build-up of tension or emotion that leads to the climax (often found in the chorus or bridge). For example, in Bob Dylan's *Tangled Up in Blue*, each verse adds a new chapter to the story, revealing different moments in a complex, shifting relationship.

For songwriters, this means thinking of the verses as **progressive steps in the narrative**. Each verse should take the listener deeper into the story, whether by revealing new information, shifting perspectives, or heightening the emotional stakes. This creates a sense of momentum, making the listener want to continue the journey to see how the story resolves. To keep the verses engaging, avoid repeating the same ideas or emotions—each verse should add something new that keeps the narrative moving forward.

CHARACTER DEVELOPMENT is another crucial element in writing verses that build a narrative. If your song features specific characters, the verses provide an opportunity to flesh out their personalities, motivations, and conflicts. By giving your characters depth and complexity, you make the song's narrative more engaging and relatable for the listener. For example, in Tracy Chapman's *Fast Car*, the verses provide a detailed, evolving portrait of the narrator's life and dreams, making the listener empathize with her struggles and aspirations.

For songwriters, this means using the verses to **develop the characters' emotions and experiences**. You might start by introducing a character's situation in the first verse, then delve deeper into their thoughts and feelings in subsequent verses. If the song is more abstract and doesn't feature specific characters, you can still use the verses to explore different facets of the emotion or theme you're addressing. By giving each verse a clear emotional or narrative progression, you create a sense of depth that keeps the listener engaged.

Tension and release are key elements of narrative-driven songwriting, and the verses play a crucial role in building tension. The verses often introduce conflicts, challenges, or questions that are resolved or addressed in the chorus. This back-and-forth between tension in the verses and release in the chorus creates a dynamic emotional journey for the listener. For example, in Adele's *Someone Like You*, the verses express longing, regret, and unresolved feelings, while the chorus offers a cathartic emotional release.

For songwriters, this means thinking about how the **emotional tension builds** throughout the verses. You can use the verses to introduce emotional conflicts or unresolved situations that lead naturally into the chorus's resolution. This technique makes the chorus feel more impactful because it serves as the emotional payoff after the build-up of tension in the verses. By carefully managing the emotional arc of the song, you ensure that the listener stays engaged with the story.

Another important aspect of writing narrative-driven verses is **using specific details and imagery** to make the story feel vivid and real. Abstract or generic lyrics can make it difficult for listeners to connect with the song on an emotional level, but concrete details bring the narrative to life. For example, in The Beatles' *Eleanor Rigby*, the verses are filled with specific details that paint a picture of loneliness and isolation: "Eleanor Rigby / Picks up the rice in the church where a wedding has been." These details give the song a sense of realism, making the emotions more immediate and relatable.

For songwriters, this means focusing on **showing rather than telling**. Instead of stating an emotion or idea outright, try to convey it through vivid imagery, actions, or specific situations. For example, rather than saying "I feel sad," you might describe a scene that captures that emotion: "The rain falls softly on an empty street, as I walk alone where we used to meet." These specific details help the listener visualize the story, making it more immersive and emotionally impactful.

PACING is another crucial factor when writing verses that build a narrative. The pacing of the verses should allow the story to unfold naturally, without rushing or dragging. If the verses move too quickly, the listener may not have time to fully engage with the narrative; if they move too slowly, the song can lose momentum. Striking the right balance ensures that the listener remains invested in the story from start to finish.

For songwriters, this means thinking carefully about how much **information or emotion to reveal in each verse**. You don't need to give everything away at once—in fact, creating a sense of mystery or anticipation can make the song more engaging. By pacing the verses to reveal new details or emotions gradually, you keep the listener hooked, eager to hear what comes next. Each verse should feel like a step forward in the story, adding new layers of meaning without overwhelming the listener.

Perspective shifts can also be a powerful tool for building a narrative through verses. Some songs use different verses to explore the same situation from multiple perspectives, creating a more layered and complex story. For example, in Dolly Parton's *Jolene*, the narrator pleads with Jolene to refrain from taking her man, giving us a one-sided view of the conflict. However, if the song had shifted perspectives—perhaps giving Jolene's point of view in a later verse—it could have deepened the emotional complexity of the narrative.

For songwriters, experimenting with **shifting perspectives** can add new dimensions to the song's narrative. You might switch between different characters, explore contrasting emotions, or even change the point of view (from first-person to third-person, for example) in different verses. This technique can create a more dynamic and engaging narrative, as the listener is exposed to multiple angles or interpretations of the same situation.

Finally, the verses should always **complement the chorus** in a narrative-driven song. While the chorus often expresses the central emotion or theme, the verses provide the context and details that make the chorus more impactful. The relationship between the verses and chorus is crucial for creating a cohesive narrative—each verse should build toward the chorus, setting up the emotional or thematic resolution that the chorus provides.

For songwriters, this means ensuring that the **verses support and enhance the chorus**. Think of the verses as the storytelling or emotional build-up that leads to the chorus's resolution. Whether you're telling a literal story or building a more abstract emotional narrative, the verses should serve as the foundation that gives the chorus its meaning and power.

In conclusion, writing verses that build a narrative requires careful attention to detail, pacing, and emotional progression. By establishing a clear setting or context, developing characters or emotions, using vivid imagery, and managing tension and release, songwriters can create verses that engage listeners and lead naturally into the chorus. Whether you're telling a specific story or exploring a broader emotional journey, the verses provide the structure and depth that make the song resonate with its audience. With the right approach, verses can transform a simple song into a powerful narrative that captivates listeners from start to finish.

Genres and Styles: What Defines Them in Songwriting

Genres and styles are essential concepts in music that help shape the identity and direction of a song. In songwriting, understanding genres and styles is crucial because they not only provide a framework for creativity but also set expectations for the listener. Genres like pop, rock, country, jazz, hip-hop, and folk have their own conventions, while various styles within these genres allow for endless creativity and flexibility. Songwriters often draw from these traditions to craft songs that feel authentic to a particular genre while also adding their own unique voice and creativity. In this chapter, we will explore what defines genres and styles in songwriting, how they shape a song's structure and sound, and how songwriters can use them as tools to enhance their craft.

The Role of Genre in Songwriting

Genre refers to a category or classification of music that shares certain characteristics, including structure, instrumentation, melody, rhythm, and lyrical themes. Each genre has its own **set of conventions** that help define its sound and style. These conventions act as guidelines for songwriters, providing a framework to work within while still allowing for personal expression and innovation. Understanding the elements that define a genre helps songwriters decide how to approach a song and what tools they can use to achieve a specific mood, emotion, or effect.

For example, in **pop music**, the focus is often on creating **catchy melodies** and **repetitive choruses** that make the song accessible and memorable. Pop songs typically feature simple, relatable lyrics, strong hooks, and an emphasis on rhythm that makes them easy to dance to or sing along with. Songs like Taylor Swift's *Shake It Off* or Dua Lipa's *Don't Start Now* follow these conventions with infectious hooks and upbeat rhythms.

In contrast, **country music** often centers around storytelling, with lyrics that focus on themes like love, heartache, small-town life, and personal struggles. Country songs tend to have **narrative-driven lyrics**, often paired with acoustic instruments like guitars, fiddles, and banjos. The simple, heartfelt delivery of artists like Johnny Cash or Dolly Parton creates an intimate connection with listeners, making the genre's emotional directness one of its key defining features.

In **rock music**, the emphasis is often on **energy, emotion, and instrumentation**. Rock songs typically feature electric guitars, bass, drums, and powerful vocals. The genre allows for both hard-hitting, rebellious songs and more introspective, emotional pieces. The structure of a rock song is often built around dynamic shifts, such as the contrast between loud, powerful choruses and softer verses. Bands like Led Zeppelin, Foo Fighters, and Nirvana exemplify how rock music balances raw energy with emotion.

Each genre comes with its own **musical vocabulary**, and songwriters often work within these established conventions to create songs that fit the genre while bringing their own unique voice. While following the conventions of a genre can help a song feel familiar and accessible, **breaking away from genre conventions** can lead to innovative and genre-defying music, which keeps the songwriter's approach fresh and exciting.

Melodic and Harmonic Structures

Melody and harmony are fundamental elements that differ across genres and help define a song's style. For example, **pop melodies** are often simple, repetitive, and easy to sing along with, while **jazz melodies** tend to be more complex, incorporating intricate phrasing and improvisation. Pop songs often use **diatonic chord progressions** (chords that stay within the same key), while **jazz songs** frequently use **chromatic chords** and **modulations** to different keys, giving the music a more unpredictable and sophisticated sound.

In genres like **folk music**, the melodies are often **rooted in tradition**, passed down through generations and emphasizing simplicity and accessibility. Folk melodies typically revolve around common chord progressions like I-IV-V, with a focus on storytelling through lyrics. Artists like Bob Dylan and Joan Baez exemplify how folk music uses simple melodies to complement powerful lyrics.

On the other hand, **classical music** and **progressive rock** explore more **complex harmonic structures** that move beyond typical pop or rock chord progressions. These genres may incorporate **modulations**, unusual time signatures, and advanced harmonic techniques, creating songs that feel more elaborate and emotionally nuanced. A band like Pink Floyd, for example, blends elements of rock with complex arrangements that defy conventional song structures, using spacey synthesizers, orchestration, and extended instrumental sections to create unique atmospheres.

Rhythm and Groove in Different Genres

Rhythm plays a central role in defining the sound and feel of a genre. In genres like **hip-hop** and **R&B**, the groove is often driven by the rhythm, with the emphasis on **beats and flow**. Hip-hop relies heavily on the rhythm of the lyrics and beats, often built around repetitive samples or drum loops. The **cadence of the lyrics** and the interaction between the rapper and the beat define the song's flow, as seen in tracks by artists like Kendrick Lamar and J. Cole. The rhythm in these genres is often syncopated, creating a sense of movement and energy that drives the song forward.

In **dance and electronic music**, the beat is central to the genre, often driven by **steady four-on-the-floor rhythms** and repetitive grooves designed to keep listeners dancing. Songs in these genres often prioritize **rhythmic consistency**, with fewer dynamic shifts than in other genres. Artists like Daft Punk and Calvin Harris create immersive rhythmic environments where the beat takes precedence over the lyrics or melody.

Conversely, in genres like **blues** and **rock**, the rhythm often takes on a more **organic** and **driving** quality, typically propelled by the drummer and bassist. Blues music, in particular, uses **shuffle rhythms** and swing patterns that give it a laid-back, soulful feel. In rock music, the rhythm section provides the backbone for high-energy performances, with faster tempos and driving beats that energize the listener.

IN **classical** and **folk music**, rhythm tends to take on a more **flexible and flowing** role, often adapting to the needs of the melody and the story being told. Folk ballads, for instance, may slow down or speed up as the narrative unfolds, giving the song a more personal and organic feel. Classical music can shift between various rhythmic patterns and time signatures within a single piece, adding complexity and emotional depth.

Lyrics and Themes

The **lyrical content** of a song also plays a major role in defining its genre. Different genres tend to focus on specific themes, and these lyrical conventions often shape the tone and message of the song. For example, **hip-hop** lyrics frequently explore themes of social justice, personal struggle, empowerment, and self-expression. Artists like Tupac Shakur and Nas use their lyrics to tell stories about their lived experiences, often addressing political and social issues.

In **country music**, lyrics often center around themes of love, heartbreak, rural life, and family values. The narrative style is deeply embedded in the genre, with songs often telling personal stories or reflecting on universal experiences like loss, longing, and nostalgia. Johnny Cash's *I Walk the Line* and Dolly Parton's *Jolene* are classic examples of country songs that tell compelling, relatable stories with straightforward, emotional lyrics.

Rock and pop lyrics can cover a wide range of themes, from love and rebellion to personal introspection and societal commentary. The flexibility of these genres allows for exploration of both lighthearted and serious topics, making them adaptable for songwriters who want to experiment with different lyrical themes.

Jazz, on the other hand, is known for its **improvisational nature**—both musically and lyrically. Jazz lyrics are often more poetic, focusing on mood, emotion, and the abstract. Jazz standards like Billie Holiday's *Strange Fruit* or Ella Fitzgerald's *Summertime* deliver poignant messages through vivid imagery, often taking on a conversational or introspective tone.

Innovation within Genre Conventions

While understanding genre conventions is important for crafting songs that fit within a particular style, many songwriters choose to **push the boundaries** of genre by blending styles or incorporating elements from multiple genres. This type of genre-blending has led to some of the most innovative and ground-breaking music in recent history. For example, artists like Prince and David Bowie defied genre conventions by blending rock, funk, pop, and soul to create entirely new sounds. In contemporary music, artists like Billie Eilish blend **pop, alternative, and electronic** elements to create songs that challenge the traditional boundaries of pop music, while artists like Lil Nas X blend **country and hip-hop** to create genre-defying hits like *Old Town Road*. This blending of genres has become more common as songwriters draw from a wide range of influences, creating new hybrid genres and expanding the possibilities for musical expression.

For songwriters, experimenting with **cross-genre elements** can be an exciting way to push your creative boundaries. By borrowing rhythmic ideas from one genre, melodic structures from another, and blending them with your own style, you can create something entirely unique. The key is to understand the conventions of each genre well enough to know when and how to break them effectively. Genres and styles play a crucial role in defining the identity of a song, shaping its structure, instrumentation, rhythm, and lyrical content. By understanding the conventions of different genres, songwriters can work within these frameworks to create songs that resonate with listeners while still allowing for personal expression and innovation. Whether you're writing a catchy pop song, a heartfelt country ballad, or an experimental genre-blending track, the tools of genre and style provide a foundation for creativity, helping you craft songs that feel authentic and emotionally impactful. Embracing and experimenting with genres can elevate your songwriting and open up new possibilities for artistic exploration.

Bridges and Transitions: Keeping the Listener's Interest

In songwriting, bridges and transitions play a critical role in keeping a song engaging and dynamic. While the verses and chorus often carry the main structure and emotional weight of a song, bridges and transitions provide variety, contrast, and a sense of progression. They break up the repetition of verses and choruses, adding a new layer of emotion, surprise, or narrative development that keeps the listener intrigued. A well-crafted bridge or seamless transition can elevate a song, helping to maintain momentum and prevent monotony. Let's explore the importance of bridges and transitions in songwriting, how they enhance a song's structure, and techniques to create effective ones.

The Role of the Bridge in Songwriting

The **bridge** is a section of a song that typically comes after the second chorus and provides a contrast to the verses and choruses. It serves as a **departure** from the established structure, offering the listener something fresh before returning to the familiar chorus or final verse. The bridge often introduces a shift in melody, harmony, lyrics, or rhythm, providing emotional or narrative development. The purpose of a bridge is to keep the listener engaged by creating a sense of change or evolution in the song, avoiding stagnation.

One of the key functions of a bridge is to **add emotional depth**. While the verses and chorus may establish the main themes and emotions of the song, the bridge allows for an exploration of new emotional territory. For example, in Adele's *Someone Like You*, the bridge provides a moment of reflection and heightened emotion, as the melody rises and the lyrics convey a deeper sense of longing and resolution. This emotional shift adds to the overall impact of the song, making the final chorus feel even more powerful.

For songwriters, the bridge offers an opportunity to **introduce a fresh perspective** or explore a new angle on the song's theme. If the verses and chorus are focused on a specific emotion or narrative, the bridge can offer a counterpoint or a new insight. For instance, in Beyoncé's *Halo*, the bridge shifts from the euphoric tone of the chorus to a more introspective and vulnerable moment, creating emotional contrast and adding depth to the song's message of love and protection.

Creating Contrast in the Bridge

One of the most effective ways to make a bridge stand out is by **creating contrast** with the rest of the song. This can be achieved through changes in melody, chord progression, dynamics, or rhythm. The contrast between the bridge and the surrounding sections helps maintain the listener's interest by introducing variety and breaking up the repetition of the verses and chorus.

IN TERMS OF **melody**, the bridge often introduces a new melodic idea that contrasts with the established melodies of the verse and chorus. This shift can create a sense of surprise or excitement, making the bridge feel like a new emotional high point. For example, in The Beatles' *We Can Work It Out*, the bridge introduces a darker, more reflective melody, contrasting with the upbeat, optimistic tone of the verse and chorus. This contrast heightens the song's emotional complexity, giving the listener a sense of tension before returning to the resolution of the chorus.

Harmonic contrast can also be an effective tool in the bridge. While the verses and chorus may use a standard chord progression, the bridge can introduce new chords or modulate to a different key, creating a sense of movement or evolution in the song. For example, in Coldplay's *Fix You*, the bridge introduces a powerful chord progression that elevates the song to a new emotional level before returning to the uplifting chorus. This harmonic shift adds depth to the song and keeps the listener engaged by taking them on an unexpected musical journey.

Dynamic shifts are another way to create contrast in the bridge. A bridge can be quieter, more introspective, or more intense and climactic than the surrounding sections, depending on the emotional arc of the song. In John Mayer's *Gravity*, the bridge builds to a powerful climax, with the instrumentation and dynamics rising to a peak before resolving back into the final chorus. This dynamic contrast makes the bridge feel like a moment of catharsis, enhancing the emotional impact of the song.

Transitions: Keeping the Song Flowing

While bridges offer contrast, **transitions** are essential for maintaining the flow and coherence of a song. Transitions help move the listener smoothly from one section of the song to another, ensuring that the shifts between verses, choruses, bridges, and outros feel natural and seamless. A well-executed transition can keep the listener engaged by preventing jarring changes that disrupt the flow of the song.

One of the most common types of transitions is the use of **pre-choruses**, which serve as a bridge between the verse and chorus. A pre-chorus often builds anticipation for the chorus by introducing a new melodic or rhythmic idea that leads naturally into the climactic chorus. For example, in Katy Perry's *Firework*, the pre-chorus builds tension with a rising melody and driving rhythm, creating a sense of anticipation before the explosive release of the chorus.

Instrumental transitions are another effective tool for keeping the listener engaged. These transitions can involve a brief instrumental break or a change in instrumentation that helps bridge the gap between sections. For example, a guitar riff, drum fill, or synth melody can serve as a transition from the verse to the chorus, adding variety while maintaining the song's momentum. In Michael Jackson's *Billie Jean*, the iconic bassline serves as a transitional element that guides the listener from the verse into the chorus, maintaining a sense of groove and continuity throughout the song.

RHYTHMIC TRANSITIONS can also be used to create a sense of flow between sections. A rhythmic change, such as a shift in tempo, time signature, or groove, can signal a transition from one part of the song to another. In Daft Punk's *Get Lucky*, the groove remains consistent throughout the song, but subtle rhythmic shifts help transition between the verse, chorus, and instrumental sections, creating a seamless flow that keeps the listener engaged on the dance floor.

Building Tension and Releasing It

One of the most powerful aspects of both bridges and transitions is their ability to **build tension and release it**. A bridge can serve as a moment of tension or contrast that makes the return to the chorus feel even more satisfying. Similarly, transitions can create anticipation by building up energy before releasing it in the next section of the song.

For example, in **Queen's** *We Are the Champions*, the bridge introduces a sense of tension through a chord progression that creates a feeling of uncertainty. This tension builds anticipation for the triumphant return to the chorus, where the resolution is fully realized. The interplay between tension and release keeps the listener emotionally engaged, making the song feel dynamic and powerful.

For songwriters, this means thinking about how you can use **musical and emotional tension** to heighten the impact of the chorus. A bridge or transition that builds tension—whether through a rising melody, dynamic shift, or harmonic change—can make the chorus feel even more powerful when it finally arrives. This technique helps maintain the listener's interest by creating a sense of movement and progression throughout the song.

Adding Layers and Complexity

Bridges and transitions also provide an opportunity to **add layers of complexity** to the song. This can involve introducing new instruments, harmonies, or textures that weren't present in the earlier sections. These additional layers help give the song a sense of evolution, making it feel more dynamic and rich.

For example, in Radiohead's *Paranoid Android*, the bridge introduces a new, slower section with layered harmonies and a different rhythmic feel. This shift adds complexity and depth to the song, transforming it from a straightforward rock song into a multi-faceted, genre-defying composition. The contrast between the sections keeps the listener on their toes, creating an unpredictable and engaging musical experience.

For songwriters, adding **layers of sound or harmony** in the bridge or transitions can create a sense of progression that enhances the overall impact of the song. Whether it's adding a vocal harmony, introducing new instrumentation, or experimenting with different textures, these layers help keep the song feeling fresh and dynamic, preventing it from becoming repetitive.

RETURNING TO THE CHORUS: The Power of Repetition

After the bridge, the return to the chorus is often one of the most powerful moments in a song. The chorus, after being contrasted with the bridge, often feels more impactful because the listener has experienced a shift in the song's dynamics or emotions. This return to the familiar chorus creates a sense of **resolution** and **emotional release**.

For example, in U2's *With or Without You*, the bridge introduces a moment of tension and build-up, with the instrumentation and dynamics gradually increasing. When the song finally returns to the chorus, it feels like a powerful release of emotion, making the final chorus even more impactful. The repetition of the chorus after the bridge reinforces its message and emotional core, giving the listener a satisfying sense of closure.

For songwriters, this means thinking about how the **bridge and chorus work together** to create an emotional arc. The bridge should provide contrast, while the return to the chorus should feel like a resolution or emotional payoff. By carefully crafting this interplay, you can create a song that feels both dynamic and cohesive, keeping the listener engaged throughout.

Bridges and transitions are essential tools in songwriting for maintaining the listener's interest and adding variety to a song's structure. A well-crafted bridge offers contrast and emotional depth, while seamless transitions ensure the song flows smoothly from one section to the next. By using techniques like contrast, tension and release, and layering, songwriters can create bridges and transitions that keep the listener engaged and elevate the overall impact of the song. Whether you're writing a pop anthem, a rock ballad, or an experimental track, mastering bridges and transitions can help you craft songs that feel dynamic, evolving, and emotionally resonant from start to finish.

Developing a Songwriting Routine: Building Consistency and Creativity

Songwriting is an art that thrives on inspiration, but it also requires discipline and structure to grow consistently. While moments of inspiration can strike unexpectedly, having a songwriting routine helps ensure that creativity becomes a habit rather than something that relies on fleeting bursts of motivation. Developing a routine allows you to work through creative blocks, improve your skills, and produce more material regularly. Whether you're an aspiring songwriter or a seasoned professional, a well-structured routine can help you harness your creativity and turn it into productive output. In this chapter, we'll explore how to develop a songwriting routine that balances discipline with creativity, helping you stay inspired while improving your craft.

The Importance of Routine in Songwriting

While it may seem counterintuitive to combine routine with creativity, establishing a **consistent schedule** for songwriting can help generate more ideas and make you a better songwriter over time. A routine provides structure and accountability, allowing you to dedicate time to your craft even when inspiration isn't flowing naturally. When you commit to writing regularly, you're more likely to tap into new ideas, experiment with different techniques, and refine your songwriting skills.

Many successful songwriters attribute their productivity to having a routine. Paul McCartney, for example, has spoken about treating songwriting like a job—sitting down to write even on days when inspiration doesn't come easily. By building songwriting into your daily or weekly schedule, you make it an integral part of your life, which helps develop the habit of writing consistently.

A songwriting routine also helps you overcome the dreaded **creative block**. Instead of waiting for inspiration, you're actively practicing and refining your craft, which makes it easier to work through difficult moments. Writing every day or setting aside dedicated time for songwriting helps demystify the process, turning songwriting from an elusive creative act into a skill that can be honed and improved with practice.

Setting Realistic Goals

To develop an effective songwriting routine, it's important to set **realistic goals** that fit your lifestyle and schedule. Trying to write a new song every day might sound ambitious, but it's often better to start with smaller, more achievable goals. For example, you could aim to write for 30 minutes each day or commit to completing one song a week. The key is to set goals that are challenging yet attainable, so you feel motivated to stick to the routine without becoming overwhelmed.

Consider breaking down your goals into **manageable steps**. Instead of aiming to write a full song in one session, focus on writing a verse, chorus, or melody. This approach makes the process feel less daunting and allows you to make progress even on days when you're not feeling particularly inspired. By setting small, achievable goals, you'll gradually build up your songwriting repertoire while avoiding burnout.

Finding the Right Time and Space

Creating a successful songwriting routine involves finding the right **time and environment** for creativity. Some songwriters work best in the morning when their minds are fresh, while others prefer writing late at night when the world is quiet. Pay attention to when you feel most creative or focused, and try to schedule your songwriting sessions during those times. Having a designated time to write helps create a sense of routine, making it easier to commit to regular practice.

In addition to finding the right time, it's important to create a **dedicated space** for songwriting. Whether it's a home studio, a quiet room, or a favorite spot outdoors, having a consistent place to write can help you get into the creative mindset. Your space should be free from distractions, so you can focus fully on the writing process. Some songwriters find inspiration in new environments, so consider experimenting with different locations if you feel stuck or uninspired.

Warming Up: Starting Your Songwriting Session

Like any creative process, songwriting often requires a **warm-up** to get your mind into a productive state. Rather than diving straight into writing a song, start with exercises that get your creativity flowing. Some useful warm-up techniques include:

- **Journaling**: Spend 5-10 minutes freewriting about anything that's on your mind. This helps clear mental clutter and allows you to focus on creative ideas.
- **Lyric brainstorming**: Write down random phrases, words, or images that come to mind. These may turn into lyrics or thematic elements later in your writing session.
- **Playing scales or improvising**: If you're a musician, warm up by playing your instrument or improvising melodies. This helps loosen your creativity and may lead to ideas for melodies or chord progressions.
- **Listening to music**: Sometimes listening to other artists' work before writing can spark inspiration. Choose a song you admire and analyze its structure, lyrics, or melody to get ideas for your own work.

The key to warming up is to allow yourself to experiment without pressure. These exercises help ease you into the creative process, making it easier to transition into writing once you feel ready.

Writing Regularly, Not Perfectly

One of the biggest challenges in developing a songwriting routine is overcoming the desire to **write perfectly** every time. When you expect every song to be a masterpiece, it's easy to feel discouraged or frustrated, especially when ideas don't come together right away. To build a productive routine, it's important to give yourself permission to **write imperfectly**. Not every song will be a hit, and that's okay. The goal of a routine is to keep you writing consistently, which will ultimately improve your skills and increase your chances of writing something great.

One technique to overcome perfectionism is to focus on **quantity over quality** in your daily or weekly sessions. Instead of obsessing over whether each lyric or melody is perfect, concentrate on getting your ideas down on paper. You can always revise later, but the key is to keep writing and generating material. The more you write, the easier it becomes to identify strong ideas and build on them. Some of your best work may emerge from a rough idea that seemed unremarkable at first.

Consider setting a **time limit** for each session to prevent yourself from overthinking or getting stuck on one section of a song. For example, you could give yourself 30 minutes to write as much as you can without stopping, then revisit your work later to refine it. This approach encourages you to focus on creativity rather than perfection, which helps you maintain momentum and productivity.

Embracing Experimentation and Growth

A songwriting routine is not just about producing songs—it's also an opportunity to **experiment** and try new techniques. As you write regularly, challenge yourself to step outside your comfort zone by exploring different genres, structures, or lyrical themes. For example, if you usually write pop songs, try experimenting with folk or jazz influences. If you typically write in a traditional verse-chorus format, challenge yourself to write a song with an unconventional structure, such as a single narrative verse with no chorus.

Experimentation helps keep your routine exciting and encourages **creative growth**. By exploring different styles and techniques, you can discover new ways of expressing yourself and avoid falling into repetitive patterns. Not every experiment will result in a finished song, but each one will help you refine your craft and develop a more versatile songwriting approach.

Revision as Part of the Routine

While the initial writing process is often the most exciting part of songwriting, **revision** is equally important for turning rough ideas into polished songs. Incorporating revision into your songwriting routine ensures that you not only generate material but also refine and improve it over time. Some songwriters dedicate certain days of the week to revising older material, while others prefer to revise immediately after completing a draft. Find a revision schedule that works for you and helps you stay consistent.

When revising, focus on **strengthening the core elements** of the song, such as the melody, lyrics, and structure. Ask yourself questions like: Does the melody feel engaging and memorable? Are the lyrics clear and emotionally resonant? Does the structure build toward a satisfying climax or resolution? Revisiting songs with fresh ears allows you to refine your work and ensure that the final product feels cohesive and polished.

It's also helpful to seek **feedback** from trusted friends, fellow songwriters, or collaborators. Sharing your work with others can provide valuable insights and help you identify areas for improvement. While it can be intimidating to share unfinished work, constructive feedback is essential for growth and can offer new perspectives that you might not have considered.

Tracking Your Progress and Staying Motivated

To maintain motivation, it's important to **track your progress** over time. Keep a journal or log where you record your songwriting sessions, noting how much you've written, what ideas you've explored, and any breakthroughs or challenges you've encountered. This allows you to see how much you've accomplished and reminds you of the progress you're making, even when it feels slow.

You can also set **milestones** to keep yourself motivated. For example, you might aim to complete 10 songs in a month or write for 20 consecutive days. Achieving these milestones provides a sense of accomplishment and helps reinforce the habit of writing regularly.

If you find yourself struggling to stay motivated, consider **changing up your routine** by introducing new challenges, collaborating with other songwriters, or setting a new goal. Sometimes a small change, like working in a different location or trying a new writing technique, can reignite your creativity and keep the routine feeling fresh.

Developing a songwriting routine is essential for building consistency, improving your craft, and staying inspired. By setting realistic goals, creating a dedicated space for writing, and embracing experimentation, you can turn songwriting into a regular habit that nurtures creativity and productivity. Remember, the key to a successful routine is to write regularly, not perfectly—allowing yourself the freedom to generate ideas without the pressure of perfection. Over time, your routine will help you overcome creative blocks, refine your skills, and produce a body of work that reflects your growth as a songwriter.

Overcoming Writer's Block: Breaking through Creative Barriers in Songwriting

Writer's block is a common challenge that every songwriter faces at some point in their creative journey. It's the frustrating feeling of staring at a blank page or an unfinished song, unsure of how to move forward. The good news is that writer's block is not a permanent state; it's a temporary hurdle that can be overcome with the right mindset and techniques. Whether you're stuck on lyrics, melody, or structure, there are strategies that can help you break through creative barriers and reignite your inspiration. In this chapter, we'll explore the causes of writer's block and practical methods for overcoming it, so you can return to your songwriting with renewed creativity and confidence.

Understanding the Causes of Writer's Block

Before diving into solutions, it's helpful to understand some of the common reasons why songwriter's block happens. Identifying the root cause can help you choose the right approach to move past it.

1. **Perfectionism**: Many songwriters struggle with the desire to make every line or melody perfect from the start. This pressure can lead to overthinking and self-criticism, preventing ideas from flowing freely. Instead of allowing the creative process to unfold naturally, perfectionism forces you to evaluate every idea too soon, stifling progress.
2. **Fear of Failure**: Similar to perfectionism, the fear of creating something "bad" can paralyze your creative process. Songwriters may worry that their ideas aren't original enough, good enough, or worthy of being heard. This fear can make it difficult to start writing or to finish a song.
3. **Lack of Inspiration**: Sometimes, writer's block is simply the result of feeling uninspired or out of ideas. Songwriters often rely on emotional experiences, life events, or musical influences for inspiration, and when those sources feel distant or absent, it can be challenging to find creative motivation.
4. **Overwhelm**: Songwriting can feel overwhelming, especially if you're working on multiple projects or trying to meet deadlines. The pressure to create something exceptional can lead to a mental block, where the weight of expectations prevents you from making any progress.

1. Shift Your Perspective: Writing without Judgment

One of the most effective ways to overcome writer's block is to **let go of the need for perfection** and focus on the act of writing itself. Instead of trying to write the perfect song from the start, allow yourself to write freely without judgment. This process, often called "freewriting," encourages you to put down any ideas that come to mind—no matter how random or unpolished they may seem.

Freewriting allows you to **explore ideas** without the pressure of getting it right. The key is to give yourself permission to write "bad" lyrics or melodies because even the roughest ideas can lead to something great. Set a timer for 10 or 15 minutes, and during that time, don't stop writing, even if you feel stuck. You might surprise yourself with what comes out once you let go of the need for perfection.

Songwriters like John Mayer and Taylor Swift have spoken about the importance of writing without judgment in the early stages of a song. By giving yourself room to create without fear, you'll be more likely to stumble upon new ideas and directions for your songs.

2. Change Your Environment

Sometimes a change of scenery can do wonders for overcoming creative blocks. If you're used to writing in the same room or environment, try moving to a new location. **Physical space** can have a big impact on creativity. Go to a park, a coffee shop, or another room in your house, and bring your notebook or instrument with you. The new surroundings can spark fresh ideas by shifting your mindset.

In addition to changing your environment, consider adding new **sensory experiences** to your writing routine. Listen to different types of music, play a new instrument, or experiment with different songwriting tools (e.g., using a loop pedal, a different tuning on your guitar, or a digital audio workstation). By stepping outside your usual habits, you'll invite fresh perspectives into your creative process.

3. Use Prompts and Limitations

If you're feeling stuck, try using **writing prompts** or **creative limitations** to spark new ideas. Sometimes, having too much freedom can be paralysing, so giving yourself specific guidelines can help narrow your focus and encourage creative thinking.

- **Word Prompts**: Use a random word generator or choose a word from a book, then write a song based on that word. You can challenge yourself to use the word in every verse or as the central theme of the chorus.
- **Chord Limitations**: Challenge yourself to write a song using only three chords. Limiting your harmonic choices can push you to get creative with your melody and lyrics.
- **Time Constraints**: Set a timer for 20 minutes and commit to writing as much as you can within that timeframe. The time pressure encourages you to focus and prevents overthinking.

Using prompts and limitations can help break the monotony of your usual process and force your brain to think differently about songwriting.

4. Collaborate with Other Songwriters

Collaboration is one of the most powerful ways to overcome writer's block. Working with another songwriter allows you to **bounce ideas off each other**, gain fresh perspectives, and approach songwriting from a different angle. Sometimes all it takes is one new idea or suggestion from a collaborator to get the creative juices flowing again.

When collaborating, don't be afraid to **experiment** and let the other person's strengths complement your own. If you're struggling with lyrics, let your co-writer focus on the words while you develop the melody or chord progression.

The key is to stay open to new ideas and not get too attached to a specific vision. Collaboration helps break the isolation of solo songwriting and can reignite your creative spark by introducing fresh energy into the process.

5. Break the Song into Smaller Parts

Sometimes writer's block happens because you're trying to tackle the entire song at once. Instead of feeling overwhelmed by the prospect of writing a full song, break it down into smaller, more manageable pieces. Focus on **one section** at a time—whether it's a verse, a chorus, or a bridge.

For example, start by writing just the **melody for the chorus** without worrying about the lyrics. Once you have the melody, move on to developing the verse. By compartmentalizing the different sections of the song, you can focus on one task at a time, making the process feel less daunting.

Another helpful technique is to **reverse the songwriting process**. If you're struggling to write a verse, try starting with the chorus or even the bridge. You might find that working backwards helps you figure out how to build the song's narrative or emotional arc in a new way.

6. Take a Break and Reset

Sometimes the best way to overcome writer's block is to **step away from the song** for a while. Forcing yourself to write when you're not feeling inspired can lead to frustration and burnout. Taking a short break allows your mind to reset and can lead to a renewed sense of creativity when you return to the song later.

Use the break to do something unrelated to music, such as going for a walk, reading a book, or engaging in a different creative activity like drawing or cooking. These activities can help **clear your mind** and give you a fresh perspective when you come back to the song. Sometimes the best ideas come when you're not actively trying to write, so give yourself permission to rest and recharge.

7. Analyze and Learn from Other Songs

When you're feeling creatively blocked, it can be helpful to **analyze songs** you admire to see how they're structured. Break down the lyrics, melody, chord progressions, and overall arrangement of a song you love. Ask yourself questions like:

- How does the song build its emotional arc?
- What makes the chorus or hook so memorable?
- How does the songwriter use repetition or variation?

By studying other songs, you can gain insight into different songwriting techniques and apply them to your own work. You might discover a new approach to writing lyrics or a different way to structure your song. This process helps you learn from successful songs and can inspire you to try new ideas in your own writing.

8. Embrace Imperfection and Keep Going

One of the most important lessons in overcoming writer's block is learning to **embrace imperfection**. Songwriting is an iterative process, and not every song will come out perfectly on the first try. Allow yourself to write bad drafts, knowing that you can always revise and improve them later. The key is to keep moving forward and not let the fear of imperfection prevent you from creating.

Every songwriter experiences writer's block at some point, but the most successful ones are those who keep writing, even through the challenges. By committing to regular practice, trying new techniques, and allowing yourself to make mistakes, you'll push through the block and come out stronger on the other side.

Writer's block is a natural part of the creative process, but it doesn't have to stop you from making progress. By shifting your perspective, using creative prompts, collaborating with others, and breaking the songwriting process into smaller parts, you can overcome the barriers that prevent you from writing. Remember, the goal is not to write perfectly every time but to keep the creative process moving forward. By embracing imperfection and staying open to new ideas, you'll find yourself breaking through writer's block and rediscovering your passion for songwriting.

Recording Demos: Bringing Your Song to Life

Recording a demo is one of the most exciting steps in the songwriting process, where you bring your song from the page to a tangible audio experience. Demos serve as the first recording of your song, capturing the essential elements—melody, lyrics, rhythm, and instrumentation—that give your music life. Whether you're recording at home with minimal equipment or in a professional studio, demos allow you to experiment with arrangement, structure, and performance before refining the final version. In this chapter, we'll explore the importance of recording demos, the tools and techniques to create effective ones, and how to use your demos as a stepping stone to a fully produced song.

The Purpose of a Demo

A **demo** is essentially a rough recording of your song, designed to capture the core elements and give a sense of how the song will sound when fully produced. The purpose of a demo is twofold: it helps you **visualize and refine** your song, and it serves as a tool to **share your music** with others—whether they are producers, collaborators, or potential listeners.

Recording a demo allows you to **hear your song come to life**, which is often very different from how it sounds in your head. It helps you identify strengths and weaknesses in the song's structure, melody, or lyrics, and gives you the opportunity to experiment with different arrangements. By listening to a demo, you can better assess what works and what needs improvement before moving forward with a polished version.

Additionally, demos are crucial if you plan to collaborate with other musicians, producers, or music industry professionals. A well-recorded demo provides a **clear vision** of your song's potential, making it easier for others to understand your artistic direction. It's a way of communicating your ideas effectively, whether you're working on arrangements with a band, pitching songs to producers, or showcasing your songwriting skills.

Choosing the Right Tools for Recording

Recording a demo doesn't require a professional studio—especially with the availability of high-quality **home recording equipment** and **digital tools**. Whether you're working with just a smartphone or a fully equipped home studio, there are a range of options for recording demos at different levels of complexity and quality.

Here are some basic tools you might need:

Digital Audio Workstation (DAW): A DAW is software that allows you to record, edit, and mix audio tracks. Popular DAWs include Logic Pro, Ableton Live, GarageBand (which is great for beginners), and Pro Tools. Each DAW has its strengths, but for demo recording, you don't need all the bells and whistles of a high-end program. Choose one that's user-friendly and fits your workflow.

Microphone: Even if you're just starting out, investing in a good-quality microphone can make a big difference in your demo recordings. A USB microphone, like the Audio-Technica ATR2100x, is a great option for beginners. For more professional sound quality, a condenser microphone like the Audio-Technica AT2020 or Shure SM7B can provide crisp, detailed recordings of vocals and acoustic instruments.

Audio Interface: An audio interface is a device that connects your microphone and instruments to your computer for recording. Some common, affordable options include the Focusrite Scarlett 2i2 and the PreSonus AudioBox. These interfaces allow for clearer and more detailed recordings than simply plugging directly into your computer.

Headphones or Monitors: To accurately hear your recordings, use studio headphones or monitor speakers. Headphones like the Audio-Technica ATH-M50x or Sony MDR-7506 are great for home recording, offering a clear and balanced sound.

Instruments: Depending on the song, you may need to record guitar, piano, bass, or other instruments. If you don't play an instrument, many DAWs include built-in **virtual instruments** that you can use to add drum loops, bass lines, or keyboard parts to your demo.

Smartphone or Portable Recorder: If you're looking for the simplest way to record a demo, a smartphone with a voice memo app can capture basic ideas quickly. This method is perfect for recording rough drafts or spontaneous ideas, though it may lack the audio quality needed for sharing with others.

Preparing to Record: Setting the Foundation

Before you begin recording your demo, it's important to **prepare your song** and **plan the arrangement**. A well-thought-out approach will make the recording process smoother and help you capture the best version of your song.

Solidify the Structure: Ensure that the song's structure is clear and cohesive before recording. Decide how many verses, choruses, and bridges you'll include, and whether there will be any instrumental sections. Even though a demo is a rough draft, it's helpful to have a **clear roadmap** of the song's flow to ensure a smooth recording process.

Plan the Arrangement: Think about which instruments you want to include in your demo. Do you want a simple acoustic recording with just guitar and vocals? Or do you want to experiment with adding bass, drums, and harmonies? Planning the arrangement beforehand helps you visualize the final sound and ensures you record each part efficiently.

Rehearse the Song: Before hitting the record button, spend time rehearsing the song. Practice your vocals, instrument parts, and transitions to ensure you feel confident and comfortable when recording. Rehearsal is especially important if you're playing multiple instruments or recording harmonies, as it will make the process smoother and more efficient.

Check Your Gear: Make sure all of your recording equipment is functioning properly before you begin. Test your microphone, audio interface, and headphones to ensure there are no technical issues. Doing a quick sound check will save you time and frustration later in the recording process.

Recording Techniques: Capturing the Best Sound

Once you're ready to record, it's important to focus on **capturing the best sound** possible, even for a demo. While demos don't need to be studio-quality, a clean and clear recording will help you—and others—hear the potential of the song more effectively.

Here are some recording tips:

1. **Start with the Core Elements**: Begin by recording the **core elements** of your song, such as the main instrument and vocals. If you're working with a band, start with the rhythm section—typically drums and bass—before layering other instruments. This foundation will help guide the rest of the arrangement.

2. **Record in Layers**: If you're recording multiple instruments or harmonies, consider recording them in **separate layers**. Start with the basic tracks—such as guitar or piano—and then gradually add vocals, harmonies, bass, and any additional elements. Recording in layers allows you to focus on one part at a time and gives you more flexibility when mixing and editing.

3. **Use Multiple Takes**: Don't be afraid to record multiple takes of each part, especially vocals. Sometimes the best performance comes after a few tries, once you've warmed up and found the right emotional delivery. Having multiple takes also gives you more options when editing, allowing you to choose the best version or even splice together different takes.

4. **Experiment with Effects**: Demos are a great opportunity to **experiment with effects** like reverb, delay, and compression. While you don't want to overuse effects, adding subtle reverb or compression can enhance the sound of your demo and make it feel more polished. If you're recording in a DAW, most have built-in effects that you can apply to vocals and instruments.

5. **Pay Attention to Levels**: Make sure that your audio levels are balanced throughout the recording. The vocals should be clear and not drowned out by the instruments, and no part of the song should be too quiet or too loud. You can adjust levels during the mixing process, but it's important to aim for balanced recordings from the start to avoid distortion or clipping.

Editing and Mixing: Refining Your Demo

Once you've recorded all the necessary parts, it's time to move on to **editing and mixing** your demo. This stage allows you to fine-tune the recording, ensuring that everything sounds cohesive and balanced.

Editing: During the editing process, you can clean up the recording by cutting out any unwanted noise or mistakes. For example, you can remove background noise, tighten up the timing of an instrumental part, or fix pitch issues in the vocals. Most DAWs have tools that allow you to make these adjustments easily.

Mixing: Mixing involves adjusting the levels of each track so that they blend together smoothly. Make sure the vocals sit prominently in the mix, while instruments like drums and bass provide a solid foundation. You can also use **EQ (equalization)** to enhance certain frequencies, such as boosting the treble for clarity or adding warmth to the low end.

Panning: Use panning to spread different instruments across the stereo field, creating a sense of space in the mix. For example, you can pan the guitar slightly to the left and the piano to the right, while keeping the vocals centered. Panning helps prevent the mix from sounding cluttered and makes each instrument more distinguishable.

Adding Effects: If you didn't add effects during the recording stage, now is the time to experiment with reverb, delay, and other effects to enhance the sound. For vocals, a touch of reverb can add depth and make them feel more present in the mix. For instruments, you can use subtle effects to add texture and atmosphere.

Sharing and Using Your Demo

Once your demo is recorded, edited, and mixed, it's time to **share it with others**. Whether you're sharing with collaborators, producers, or potential listeners, your demo serves as a tool to showcase the essence of your song and gather feedback.

1. **Collaborators and Producers**: If you're working with a producer or collaborating with other musicians, a demo provides a **starting point** for the arrangement and production. It allows others to hear your ideas and contribute their own suggestions for how to improve the song.
2. **Pitching to Artists or Labels**: If you're a songwriter looking to pitch your songs to artists, publishers, or labels, a well-recorded demo can help you make a strong impression. While it doesn't need to be fully produced, the demo should clearly convey the potential of the song and showcase your songwriting skills.
3. **Personal Reference**: A demo also serves as a personal reference for you as you continue to develop the song. Listening back to the demo allows you to assess what works and what doesn't, helping you refine the lyrics, melody, or arrangement before moving on to a final version.

Recording demos is an essential part of the songwriting process, bringing your song to life and allowing you to hear it in a tangible form. Whether you're working with minimal equipment or recording in a home studio, the goal of a demo is to capture the essence of your song and provide a foundation for further refinement. By focusing on preparation, recording techniques, and effective editing, you can create demos that not only showcase your songwriting but also serve as a valuable tool for collaboration and feedback. Ultimately, a well-crafted demo can help you take your song to the next stage, transforming it from an idea into a fully realized piece of music.

Marketing Your Music: Getting Heard

Creating great music is only part of the journey for any songwriter or musician—the next challenge is getting your music heard by the right audience. In today's digital age, independent artists have more opportunities than ever to promote and distribute their music, but the abundance of platforms and channels can make it difficult to know where to start. Effective marketing is essential to ensure that your songs reach their full potential and resonate with a broader audience. From building a strong online presence to leveraging streaming platforms, social media, and live performances, marketing your music requires both creativity and strategy. In this chapter, we'll explore the key steps to market your music successfully and grow your fanbase.

Building Your Brand as an Artist

Before you start marketing your music, it's important to have a clear sense of your **artist identity** or **brand**. Your brand represents who you are as an artist, your unique sound, style, and the message you want to communicate through your music. A strong brand helps you stand out in a crowded marketplace and gives fans something to connect with beyond the music itself.

1. **Define Your Sound and Message**: Start by identifying the core elements of your music—your genre, influences, and themes. What emotions or ideas do you want to convey through your songs? What makes your sound unique? Having a clear sense of your musical identity will help guide your marketing efforts, from your visuals to your social media presence.
2. **Create a Visual Identity**: Along with your sound, your **visual identity** plays a significant role in how you present yourself to the world. This includes your artist logo, album artwork, and the imagery you use in music videos and social media posts. Consistency in your visuals helps reinforce your brand and makes it easier for fans to recognize your work.
3. **Develop Your Story**: Every successful artist has a compelling story that connects with their audience. Whether it's your personal journey, the inspiration behind your music, or the message you want to share with the world, your story adds depth to your brand and helps fans relate to you on a deeper level. Share your story through interviews, social media, and your website to create a more personal connection with your audience.

Leveraging Social Media

Social media is one of the most powerful tools for promoting your music and building a fanbase. It allows you to reach a global audience, engage directly with fans, and share your music instantly. However, successful social media marketing requires more than just posting randomly—you need a **consistent strategy** that aligns with your goals as an artist.

1. **Choose the Right Platforms**: Focus on the platforms where your target audience is most active. For musicians, platforms like **Instagram**, **TikTok**, **YouTube**, and **Twitter** are especially effective for engaging with fans and sharing music content. Each platform has its own strengths—Instagram is great for visual storytelling and behind-the-scenes content, while TikTok excels at viral challenges and short-form music clips.
2. **Engage Consistently**: Post regularly to keep your fans engaged and your music top of mind. This doesn't mean bombarding your followers with content every hour, but aim for a consistent schedule—whether it's posting daily, several times a week, or releasing new music clips, teasers, or updates on a regular basis. Keep your fans in the loop about your creative process, upcoming releases, live performances, and personal stories.
3. **Create Shareable Content**: Use social media to create content that your fans will want to share. This could include behind-the-scenes videos, acoustic performances, music challenges, or sneak peeks of new songs. **Collaborating** with other artists or influencers can also help you reach new audiences and build connections with potential fans.
4. **Engage with Your Audience**: Social media is a two-way street. Responding to comments, messages, and fan interactions shows that you appreciate their support and fosters a sense of community. The more you engage with your followers, the more likely they are to stay invested in your music and share it with others.
5. **Use Hashtags and Trends**: Leverage popular hashtags and trends to make your content more discoverable. On platforms like TikTok and Instagram, using trending hashtags or participating in viral challenges can help your music reach a wider audience. However, always stay authentic and make sure the trends align with your brand and music.

Streaming Platforms: Reaching a Global Audience

With the rise of platforms like **Spotify**, **Apple Music**, and **YouTube Music**, streaming has become the dominant way people discover and consume music. Getting your music on these platforms is essential for reaching a global audience and growing your fanbase.

Distribute Your Music: To get your songs on major streaming platforms, use a **digital distribution service** like DistroKid, TuneCore, or CD Baby. These services upload your music to streaming platforms and help you collect royalties from streams. Make sure your tracks are properly tagged with accurate metadata, including song title, artist name, and genre, so they're easily discoverable by listeners.

Create a Spotify Artist Profile: On Spotify, you can create a **Spotify for Artists** profile, which gives you access to tools that help you manage your artist presence, track your performance metrics, and connect with fans. Customize your profile with your bio, photos, and links to social media, and use it as a hub to promote your latest releases.

Submit to Playlists: One of the most effective ways to gain exposure on streaming platforms is by getting your music featured on **playlists**. While official playlists curated by Spotify editors can be competitive, independent playlists curated by influencers or fans are a great way to start. Use services like SubmitHub or Playlist Push to pitch your songs to playlist curators, or reach out directly to curators on social media.

Encourage Fans to Stream and Share: Encourage your fans to add your songs to their personal playlists and share them with friends. Streaming platforms often use **algorithms** that reward engagement—so the more your songs are streamed, saved, or shared, the more likely they are to be recommended to new listeners.

Monitor Your Analytics: Most streaming platforms provide **analytics** that show how your songs are performing, including data on streams, demographics, and listener behavior. Use these insights to understand your audience better, identify which songs are resonating the most, and refine your marketing efforts based on the data.

Building an Email List: Direct Connection with Fans

While social media is great for engaging with fans, building an **email list** is one of the most valuable tools for maintaining a direct connection with your audience. Unlike social media algorithms, which can limit the reach of your posts, email allows you to reach your fans directly and keep them informed about your latest releases, tours, and updates.

1. **Offer an Incentive**: Encourage fans to sign up for your email list by offering something exclusive, such as a free download of a song, early access to a music video, or a discount on merch. Make it easy to sign up by embedding a form on your website, social media pages, or streaming profiles.
2. **Send Regular Updates**: Use your email list to send **regular newsletters** with updates about your music, upcoming shows, or behind-the-scenes content. Keep the tone personal and engaging—your email list is a direct line to your most dedicated fans, so use it to build a deeper connection with them.
3. **Promote New Releases**: When you release new music, use your email list to announce it to your subscribers. Include links to your streaming platforms, music videos, or merch, and encourage your fans to share the release with their friends. Your email list is a powerful tool for driving streams, sales, and engagement.

Music Videos and Visual Content

Music videos and visual content are an integral part of promoting your music, especially in today's visually driven digital world. A great music video can not only showcase your song but also strengthen your brand and help you connect with your audience on a deeper level.

1. **Create Engaging Music Videos**: Whether you're working with a professional production team or shooting on a budget, a well-crafted music video can make your song more memorable and shareable. Use the video to visually express the emotion or story behind your song, and share it across platforms like YouTube, Instagram, and TikTok to reach a wider audience.
2. **Leverage YouTube**: YouTube is the second-largest search engine in the world and a critical platform for discovering new music. Uploading your music videos, lyric videos, or even live performances to YouTube can help you reach new fans. Use **keywords** and SEO (search engine optimization) techniques in your video titles and descriptions to make your videos more discoverable.
3. **Short-Form Video Content**: Platforms like TikTok and Instagram Reels have popularized **short-form video content**, which can be a powerful tool for promoting snippets of your music. Create short, engaging clips of your songs, whether it's a performance, behind-the-scenes footage, or a visual challenge that encourages fan participation.

Performing Live and Building Local Support

While digital marketing is essential, **live performances** remain one of the best ways to build a dedicated fanbase and create lasting connections with your audience. Performing live allows fans to experience your music in a personal and engaging way, and it gives you the chance to showcase your skills and stage presence.

1. **Book Local Gigs**: Start by performing at local venues, open mics, or festivals to build a following in your hometown. Local gigs help you develop your live performance skills while also creating a grassroots fanbase. As you gain experience and recognition, you can start booking shows at larger venues or even plan regional tours.
2. **Engage with Your Audience**: When performing live, take the time to **connect with your audience** both on and off stage. Introduce yourself, share the stories behind your songs, and engage with fans after the show. Building a personal connection with your audience can turn casual listeners into loyal supporters who will continue to follow your music journey.
3. **Sell Merchandise**: Live shows are also a great opportunity to sell merchandise like T-shirts, posters, or physical copies of your music. Merch sales not only help support your music financially but also serve as a way for fans to represent and promote your brand.

Paid Advertising and Promotions

In addition to organic marketing strategies, **paid advertising** can be an effective way to reach a broader audience, especially when promoting new releases or tours. Platforms like **Facebook Ads**, **Instagram Ads**, and **YouTube Ads** allow you to target specific demographics, locations, and interests, ensuring your music reaches the right listeners.

1. **Target Your Audience**: Use advertising tools to define your target audience based on factors like age, location, and musical preferences. For example, if you're a pop artist, you might target fans of similar artists within your genre. Paid ads can help you promote new releases, grow your social media following, or sell tickets to upcoming shows.
2. **Boost Social Media Posts**: Many social media platforms allow you to **boost posts**, making them visible to a larger audience beyond your followers. This can be especially useful when promoting a new music video, single, or album.
3. **Track Your ROI**: Paid advertising can be an investment, so it's important to track the **return on investment (ROI)**. Use analytics to monitor how your ads are performing and adjust your strategy based on the results. Focus on campaigns that drive engagement, such as streams, downloads, or social media interactions.

Marketing your music is an essential part of getting heard in today's competitive music industry. By building a strong artist brand, leveraging social media and streaming platforms, engaging directly with fans, and performing live, you can create a comprehensive marketing strategy that helps you reach a wider audience. While the process requires dedication and creativity, the key to success is consistency and authenticity—staying true to your unique sound and vision while continuously engaging with your growing fanbase. With the right approach, you can take your music beyond the studio and into the ears and hearts of listeners around the world.

Using Social Media to Promote Your Songs: Connecting with Fans and Building Your Audience

Social media has transformed the way musicians promote their songs, allowing artists to connect directly with fans, share their music instantly, and build a global audience. Platforms like Instagram, TikTok, YouTube, and Twitter have become essential tools for promoting music, offering endless opportunities for discovery and engagement. However, successfully using social media to promote your songs requires more than just posting links to your music—you need a strategy that engages your audience, builds your brand, and creates a community around your music. In this chapter, we'll explore how to effectively use social media to promote your songs, grow your fanbase, and keep your audience engaged.

The Role of Social Media in Music Promotion

Social media is an indispensable tool for musicians in today's music industry. It gives you the ability to **reach a global audience**, connect directly with fans, and share your music in real-time. Whether you're releasing a new song, promoting a live performance, or simply sharing behind-the-scenes content, social media allows you to interact with your audience on a personal level.

The key to successful social media promotion is **engagement**. Social media isn't just about broadcasting your music—it's about creating a dialogue with your fans, building a community, and giving your audience a reason to keep coming back. This means being consistent, authentic, and strategic with your posts.

Choosing the Right Platforms

Not all social media platforms are created equal, and each one offers unique opportunities for music promotion. It's important to focus your efforts on the platforms where your target audience is most active and where your music is likely to resonate.

Instagram: Instagram is one of the most popular platforms for musicians, thanks to its visual focus and storytelling capabilities. Use Instagram to post photos and videos, share behind-the-scenes content, and promote new releases through Instagram Stories, Reels, and IGTV. The platform's use of **hashtags** makes it easier for new listeners to discover your music.

TikTok: TikTok has become a powerhouse for music promotion, with many songs going viral through short-form videos and challenges. Use TikTok to create engaging music clips, start trends, and encourage fans to participate in challenges using your song. TikTok's **algorithm** favors viral content, so even a relatively unknown artist can gain massive exposure if a video resonates with the platform's users.

YouTube: YouTube is essential for music videos, lyric videos, and live performances. It's also a great platform for **long-form content** like behind-the-scenes footage or vlogs. Creating a YouTube channel allows you to build a library of video content that can be monetized through ads and shared across other platforms.

Twitter: Twitter is a great platform for **real-time interaction** with your fans. Use it to share quick updates, engage in conversations, and build relationships with your audience. Twitter is also an excellent platform for **promoting upcoming shows** or releases, using hashtags to reach a broader audience.

Facebook: While Facebook is no longer the primary platform for many younger music fans, it's still valuable for building a community, especially through **Facebook groups** and **events**. Use Facebook to promote your music, live shows, and other events, and engage with fans through comments and messages.

Twitch: If you're interested in **live streaming**, Twitch is an ideal platform for hosting virtual concerts, live Q&A sessions, or even songwriting sessions. Live interaction creates a real-time connection with your audience, allowing fans to feel more involved in your creative process.

Creating a Consistent Posting Schedule

One of the most important aspects of using social media to promote your songs is consistency. **Posting regularly** helps keep your music and brand visible, ensures that you stay top-of-mind for your followers, and increases the likelihood of your content being shared and discovered by new fans.

1. **Establish a Posting Schedule**: Decide how often you want to post on each platform. For Instagram and TikTok, posting at least a few times a week is ideal, while platforms like Twitter may require more frequent posts to stay relevant in fast-moving conversations. Consistency is key, so stick to a schedule that works for you without overwhelming yourself.
2. **Plan Your Content**: Use a **content calendar** to plan your posts in advance. This allows you to coordinate content around important events like song releases, live shows, or music video premieres. Planning ahead also helps you maintain a steady flow of content, ensuring that you're regularly engaging with your audience.
3. **Balance Promotional and Personal Content**: While it's important to promote your music, be careful not to overwhelm your followers with promotional posts. Social media users value **authenticity**, so mix promotional content with personal, behind-the-scenes posts that give fans a glimpse into your life as an artist. This balance helps build a deeper connection with your audience and keeps your content engaging.

Engaging Your Audience

Engagement is the key to building a loyal fanbase on social media. Rather than just promoting your music, focus on **creating a dialogue** with your audience. Engaging directly with your fans helps build a community around your music and encourages listeners to become more invested in your career.

1. **Respond to Comments and Messages**: Take the time to reply to comments on your posts and respond to direct messages from fans. Engaging with your followers makes them feel valued and helps create a personal connection. The more you interact with your fans, the more likely they are to share your music and promote it within their own social circles.
2. **Use Polls and Q&A Sessions**: Platforms like Instagram and Twitter allow you to create polls and host Q&A sessions, which are great ways to engage your audience. Ask your followers about their favorite songs, what they'd like to see next, or any questions they have about your music. This interactive content helps you learn more about your audience and builds excitement around your music.
3. **Go Live**: Hosting a **live session** on Instagram, Facebook, or Twitch allows you to interact with your fans in real time. Live sessions can include acoustic performances, song requests, Q&A sessions, or even a behind-the-scenes look at your songwriting or recording process. Live streaming helps create a sense of intimacy and immediacy, allowing fans to feel more connected to your creative journey.
4. **Create Challenges and Contests**: Encourage fan participation by creating **challenges or contests** around your music. For example, you could start a TikTok dance challenge using your song, or host a fan art contest on Instagram. Challenges encourage your followers to engage with your music in creative ways and share it with their own networks, helping your music reach a broader audience.

Promoting New Releases

When releasing new music, social media is your most powerful tool for building anticipation and driving traffic to your new song. Here are some strategies for **effectively promoting new releases** on social media:

Tease the Release: Build anticipation for your new song by posting **teasers** in the weeks leading up to the release. This could include a snippet of the song, a sneak peek at the album art, or a behind-the-scenes video of the recording process. Teasing the release helps create excitement and ensures that your followers are ready to stream or purchase the song as soon as it drops.

Create a Countdown: Use Instagram Stories or other platforms to create a **countdown** leading up to the release date. Countdowns help build anticipation and give your audience something to look forward to. You can also use the countdown as an opportunity to share exclusive content or offer pre-release downloads.

Launch a Pre-Save Campaign: If your music is available on streaming platforms like Spotify, launch a **pre-save campaign** to encourage fans to add your song to their libraries before it's released. Pre-saves can boost your song's visibility on release day and help it gain momentum on streaming platforms.

Use Hashtags and Tag Influencers: When promoting a new release, use relevant **hashtags** to increase the visibility of your posts. Hashtags help your music reach new listeners who may not already be following you. Additionally, if there are influencers or industry professionals who might be interested in your music, tag them in your posts to increase the chances of your song being shared more widely.

Post-Release Engagement: After your song is released, continue promoting it by sharing behind-the-scenes stories about the song's creation, lyric breakdowns, or fan reactions. Encourage your fans to share the song on their own profiles and playlists, and engage with posts that mention your new release. Keeping the momentum going after the release is just as important as building anticipation beforehand.

Leveraging User-Generated Content

One of the most powerful forms of social media promotion is **user-generated content (UGC)**. When your fans share your music on their own profiles—whether by using your song in a TikTok video, posting a cover of it on YouTube, or sharing a concert photo on Instagram—it amplifies your reach and helps introduce your music to new audiences.

1. **Encourage Fans to Share**: Encourage your fans to create their own content using your songs. You could ask them to share covers, dance videos, or artwork inspired by your music. Use hashtags to make it easier for you to find and repost user-generated content, and consider offering shout-outs or small prizes as an incentive.
2. **Repost Fan Content**: Reposting UGC on your own social media accounts not only shows appreciation for your fans but also encourages more people to create content around your music. Whether it's a fan cover or a post about your latest single, sharing their content helps build a stronger connection with your audience and fosters a sense of community.
3. **Create Challenges and Campaigns**: Platforms like TikTok are built around **viral challenges** that encourage users to create their own versions of popular trends. Starting a challenge based on your song—whether it's a dance, a lip-sync, or a creative video—can help your music gain viral momentum and reach new listeners.

Analytics: Measuring Your Success

Social media platforms offer built-in **analytics tools** that allow you to track the performance of your posts and understand how your audience is engaging with your content. Use these tools to measure the success of your social media efforts and adjust your strategy accordingly.

1. **Track Engagement**: Monitor how many likes, comments, shares, and views your posts receive. High engagement rates indicate that your content is resonating with your audience. Pay attention to which types of posts perform best and use that information to refine your content strategy.
2. **Analyze Follower Growth**: Keep track of your follower count over time and note any spikes in growth, especially after promoting new releases or engaging with fans. Understanding what drives follower growth helps you identify which strategies are most effective.
3. **Review Click-Through Rates**: If you're promoting your music on streaming platforms, monitor the **click-through rates** on links you post. This data helps you see how many people are following through from your social media posts to stream or purchase your music.
4. **Refine Your Strategy**: Use the insights from your analytics to refine your social media strategy. If you notice that certain types of content—like live performances or behind-the-scenes videos—receive more engagement, focus on creating more of that content. Continually adapt your approach based on what resonates with your audience.

Social media is a powerful tool for promoting your songs and connecting with fans, but it requires a thoughtful and consistent strategy to be effective. By choosing the right platforms, engaging with your audience, promoting new releases creatively, and leveraging user-generated content, you can build a loyal fanbase and increase the reach of your music. The key to success on social media is authenticity—by sharing your unique voice and connecting with fans in a genuine way, you'll create a lasting impact and grow your music career in meaningful ways.

Leveraging YouTube to Showcase Your Talent: Building an Audience Through Video Content

YouTube has become one of the most influential platforms for musicians and artists to showcase their talent. As the second-largest search engine in the world, YouTube offers unparalleled opportunities for musicians to reach global audiences, build a dedicated fanbase, and share their work with a visually engaging medium. Whether you're posting music videos, live performances, covers, or behind-the-scenes content, YouTube allows you to create a multimedia experience that complements your music. In this chapter, we'll explore how to leverage YouTube to showcase your talent, create engaging content, and grow your audience.

The Importance of YouTube for Musicians

YouTube is not just a platform for uploading videos—it's a powerful tool for **discoverability, promotion, and engagement**. For musicians, it offers a space to share not only your music but also your personality, creative process, and visual identity. YouTube allows you to:

1. **Reach a Global Audience**: With billions of active users, YouTube enables you to connect with listeners from all over the world. Whether you're an independent artist or a signed musician, YouTube offers the potential for your videos to be discovered by new fans through search, recommendations, and social sharing.
2. **Build Your Brand**: Your YouTube channel serves as a hub for your music and content, giving you a platform to showcase your artistic vision. From music videos to vlogs, YouTube allows you to shape your visual and musical identity, helping you build a cohesive brand that resonates with your audience.
3. **Monetize Your Content**: In addition to promoting your music, YouTube offers monetization options through the **YouTube Partner Program**, which allows you to earn revenue from ads placed on your videos. While this may not be a primary source of income at first, as your channel grows, YouTube can become a valuable revenue stream.
4. **Engage with Fans**: YouTube's comment section, community tab, and live streaming features allow you to engage directly with your audience. Building a community on YouTube helps create loyal fans who are invested not only in your music but in your journey as an artist.

Creating a YouTube Channel That Stands Out

Your YouTube channel is the foundation for showcasing your talent, so it's important to create a channel that is professional, engaging, and reflective of your brand.

1. **Channel Name and Branding**: Choose a channel name that reflects your artist name or band name for consistency. Your branding should align with your overall artistic identity—this includes your **profile picture**, **banner art**, and **channel description**. Use high-quality images and a description that introduces who you are, your genre, and what viewers can expect from your content.
2. **Organize Your Content**: As you upload more videos, organize them into **playlists** to make it easier for viewers to navigate your channel. You can create playlists for official music videos, live performances, cover songs, and behind-the-scenes content. This not only makes your channel more user-friendly but also encourages viewers to watch more of your content.
3. **Optimize Your Videos for SEO**: YouTube is a search engine, so optimizing your videos for **search engine optimization (SEO)** is crucial for discoverability. Use relevant keywords in your video titles, descriptions, and tags to increase the chances of your videos appearing in search results. For example, if you're posting a cover of a popular song, include the song title, artist name, and relevant keywords like "acoustic cover" in the title and description.
4. **Engage with Your Audience**: Encourage viewers to **subscribe** to your channel, like your videos, and leave comments. The more engagement your videos receive, the more likely they are to be recommended to new viewers. Respond to comments and use the **community tab** to post updates, polls, and behind-the-scenes content, helping to foster a deeper connection with your audience.

Types of Content to Showcase Your Talent

To effectively leverage YouTube, it's important to create a variety of content that showcases your musical skills while keeping your audience engaged. Here are some types of videos that can help you build your channel and connect with fans:

Music Videos: Music videos are the most obvious way to showcase your songs on YouTube. Whether you produce a high-budget video or a simple, artistic visual, a well-crafted music video can bring your song to life and help create a memorable experience for listeners. Music videos are also highly shareable, making them a great way to promote your music across other social media platforms.

Lyric Videos: If you're unable to create a full music video, lyric videos are a great alternative. They allow you to visually represent your song while highlighting your lyrics. Many fans appreciate lyric videos because they allow listeners to follow along with the words and connect more deeply with the song's meaning.

Live Performances: Posting live performance videos helps showcase your musicianship and stage presence. Whether you're recording a performance at a venue, streaming a live concert, or doing an intimate acoustic session from your home, live performances offer fans a raw and authentic version of your music.

Covers of Popular Songs: Covering well-known songs is a great way to gain exposure and introduce new listeners to your channel. Many artists have grown their fanbase by posting creative renditions of popular songs. When choosing songs to cover, consider what's trending, but also make sure to choose songs that align with your musical style so you can add your own unique twist.

Behind-the-Scenes Content: Sharing behind-the-scenes videos gives your audience insight into your creative process. Whether you're in the studio recording a new track, rehearsing with your band, or preparing for a music video shoot, behind-the-scenes content allows fans to feel more connected to your journey as an artist.

Vlogs and Personal Updates: In addition to music-related content, posting **vlogs** or personal updates helps build a more personal connection with your audience. You could talk about your experiences as a musician, share stories about your songwriting process, or offer insights into your daily life. This type of content helps humanize you as an artist and makes fans feel more invested in your journey.

Collaborations: Collaborating with other musicians, influencers, or YouTubers is a great way to expand your reach and grow your audience. You could collaborate on a cover, create original music together, or even appear as a guest on each other's channels. Collaborations allow you to tap into each other's fanbases, increasing visibility for both parties.

Tutorials and Educational Content: If you have expertise in music production, songwriting, or playing instruments, consider posting **tutorials** or educational content. Teaching your audience how to play one of your songs or sharing tips on songwriting can position you as an authority in your field while also attracting new viewers who are interested in learning.

Growing Your YouTube Channel

Once you've started uploading content, the key to growing your YouTube channel is consistency, engagement, and promotion.

Consistency is Key: Posting videos regularly helps keep your channel active and increases the likelihood of your content being recommended to new viewers. Develop a posting schedule—whether it's weekly or biweekly—and stick to it. Let your audience know when to expect new content so they can look forward to your uploads.

Promote Your Videos on Social Media: Cross-promote your YouTube videos on all of your social media platforms, including Instagram, Twitter, Facebook, and TikTok. Sharing clips or teasers from your videos can drive traffic to your channel. Encourage your followers to subscribe, like, and share your content to help spread the word.

Use Thumbnails and Titles Strategically: Your video thumbnails and titles are the first things viewers see, so make them eye-catching and descriptive. Use high-quality images for your thumbnails and add text that gives viewers a sense of what to expect. Your titles should include relevant keywords while still being engaging—avoid clickbait but aim to pique curiosity.

Engage with Your Community: Building a community on YouTube is just as important as posting content. Reply to comments on your videos, ask viewers for feedback, and engage with your audience through polls or community posts. The more you interact with your fans, the more likely they are to stay loyal and spread the word about your channel.

Collaborate with YouTubers and Influencers: As mentioned earlier, collaborations can significantly boost your channel's visibility. Consider reaching out to other YouTubers or influencers in your niche and proposing a collaboration. Whether it's a joint cover, a Q&A session, or a live performance, collaborating can introduce your channel to a wider audience.

Optimize for Watch Time: YouTube's algorithm favors videos with longer watch times, so aim to create content that keeps viewers engaged for as long as possible. Consider breaking up longer content into series or multi-part videos to encourage viewers to watch more of your content. Creating engaging intros and keeping your videos focused will also help retain viewers' attention.

Monetize Your Channel: Once your channel reaches 1,000 subscribers and 4,000 watch hours in the past 12 months, you can apply to the **YouTube Partner Program** and start earning ad revenue from your videos. While this won't be a primary income stream at first, it's a great way to monetize your content as your channel grows.

Utilizing YouTube Live for Real-Time Engagement

In addition to uploading pre-recorded content, YouTube Live is a powerful way to engage with your audience in real time. Whether you're hosting a live performance, doing a Q&A session, or simply chatting with fans, live streaming helps build a sense of community and intimacy with your audience.

Host Live Performances: Use YouTube Live to perform acoustic sets, full concerts, or even debut new songs. Live performances create a unique experience for your viewers and allow them to interact with you directly through the live chat.

Q&A Sessions: Hosting live Q&A sessions is a great way to connect with your audience and answer their questions about your music, creative process, or upcoming projects. You can also use these sessions to gather feedback or ideas from your fans.

Promote Your Live Streams: Make sure to promote your live streams across your social media platforms in advance, giving your audience plenty of notice so they can tune in. You can also schedule your live streams directly on YouTube so viewers can set reminders to join when you go live.

Engage During the Stream: Interacting with viewers in the chat during the live stream makes the experience more engaging and personal. Shout out fans who comment, respond to their questions, and make them feel like they're part of the experience.

YouTube is a powerful platform for showcasing your talent and building a dedicated fanbase. By creating a variety of engaging content—such as music videos, live performances, covers, and behind-the-scenes footage—you can grow your audience and build your brand as an artist. Consistency, engagement, and strategic promotion are key to leveraging YouTube effectively.

Selling Your Songs Online: Platforms and Strategies

In today's digital world, musicians and songwriters have more opportunities than ever to sell their songs online, reaching a global audience without needing a traditional record label or distributor. Whether you're an independent artist looking to monetize your music or a songwriter offering songs to other performers, the internet provides numerous platforms and strategies to sell your work. However, navigating the various platforms and understanding how to maximize your sales potential requires careful planning and marketing. In this chapter, we'll explore the best platforms for selling your songs online, as well as effective strategies to boost your sales and reach a wider audience.

The Benefits of Selling Songs Online

Before diving into specific platforms, it's important to understand the benefits of selling your music online. Unlike traditional distribution methods, online sales provide:

1. **Global Reach**: Selling your songs online allows you to reach listeners from all over the world, expanding your audience beyond your local market.
2. **Creative Control**: As an independent artist, you maintain full control over your music, brand, and pricing, ensuring your songs are presented exactly as you envision them.
3. **Higher Profit Margins**: Without the need for a record label or physical distribution, you can keep a larger share of the revenue from each sale or stream.
4. **Direct Connection with Fans**: Selling your songs online allows you to build a direct relationship with your fans, offering opportunities for engagement, loyalty, and continued support.

Choosing the Right Platforms to Sell Your Songs

There are various platforms designed to help musicians sell their songs online, each offering unique features and benefits. When choosing a platform, consider factors such as distribution reach, pricing options, and the platform's ease of use.

Bandcamp

Bandcamp is a popular platform for independent musicians to sell their music directly to fans. It allows you to sell digital downloads, physical merchandise (such as vinyl and CDs), and even special edition releases. Bandcamp is particularly artist-friendly, as it allows you to set your own prices, including offering "pay-what-you-want" pricing, which encourages fan support.

Benefits:

You keep a significant portion of sales revenue (Bandcamp takes only a small fee).

Fans can support you by paying more than the set price if they choose.

Easy to sell both digital and physical products.

Strategies:

Offer exclusive content, such as bonus tracks or limited-edition merchandise, to incentivize purchases.

Use Bandcamp's built-in fan messaging to stay connected with your audience and update them on new releases.

Apple Music / iTunes

Selling your music on **Apple Music** (formerly iTunes) allows you to reach one of the largest audiences of music buyers. You can sell individual songs, albums, or offer special bundles. While Apple Music has shifted its focus to streaming, many listeners still purchase downloads through the iTunes Store.

Benefits:

Access to a large, established audience.

Integration with Apple's ecosystem for easy discovery and promotion.

Strategies:

Use Apple Music's pre-order option to build anticipation for your upcoming releases.

Promote your music through Apple's playlist curation services, which can help you reach new listeners.

Spotify

While **Spotify** is primarily known for streaming, it offers artists the chance to sell **merchandise** and other products through integrations with platforms like **Shopify**. Though you don't sell individual songs on Spotify, the exposure you gain through streaming can lead to sales on other platforms and create opportunities for merchandise sales.

Benefits:

Huge global reach and visibility.

Integration with third-party platforms for selling merch.

Strategies:

Use Spotify for Artists to track analytics and understand where your listeners are coming from, helping you target specific regions or demographics.

Promote upcoming releases through Spotify's playlist submission process to increase exposure.

AMAZON MUSIC

Amazon Music allows you to sell your songs digitally to millions of users worldwide. Similar to Apple Music, Amazon offers both streaming and digital download services. With Amazon Music, you can sell your music through the **Amazon Digital Music Store**, making it accessible to Amazon's massive customer base.

Benefits:

Access to Amazon's large customer base and built-in discovery features.

Easy integration with other Amazon services, such as physical product sales.

Strategies:

Use Amazon's "CreateSpace" service to sell physical copies of your albums.

Utilize Amazon's advertising services to promote your music to a targeted audience.

DistroKid / TuneCore / CD Baby

These platforms act as **music distribution services**, allowing you to sell your music across various platforms such as Apple Music, Spotify, Amazon Music, and more. For a fee, these services handle the logistics of distributing your music, making it available on multiple digital storefronts and streaming services.

Benefits:

Wide distribution across major streaming and download platforms.

Easy to manage distribution from a single dashboard.

Strategies:

Use DistroKid's **hyperfollow** link to direct all traffic to one place when promoting your music across different platforms.

Offer exclusive tracks or remixes on one platform while distributing the core release more widely.

SoundCloud

SoundCloud allows artists to upload, share, and sell their music directly through its platform. While primarily used for streaming, SoundCloud offers **fan-powered royalties**, where artists can earn revenue based on fan engagement and monetized streams.

Benefits:

Built-in fanbase for discovering new music.

Ability to interact directly with listeners through comments and messages.

Strategies:

Upload demos, remixes, or early versions of songs to build excitement for official releases.

Engage with listeners through SoundCloud's interactive features to encourage support and sales.

Maximizing Sales and Engagement

Simply uploading your songs to an online platform isn't enough—you need to actively promote your music and engage with your audience to maximize sales. Here are some strategies to help you effectively sell your songs online:

Offer Exclusive Content

To incentivize fans to purchase your songs instead of streaming them, offer **exclusive content** that can't be found elsewhere. This could include bonus tracks, remixes, live versions, or behind-the-scenes videos. Offering special editions of your albums, limited-time releases, or exclusive physical merchandise can create a sense of urgency and value for fans.

Build a Strong Social Media Presence

Use your social media platforms (Instagram, TikTok, YouTube, Facebook) to promote your songs and direct traffic to your sales platform. Regularly engage with your audience, share updates about new releases, and use social media to **tease new music** with snippets, music videos, or live performances.

Encourage your followers to **pre-save** or **pre-order** your songs before they are released.

Use hashtags, collaborations, and giveaways to boost visibility.

Create a Website with Direct Sales

Having your own **website** allows you to sell music directly to fans without going through third-party platforms that take a cut of your profits. Use an e-commerce platform like Shopify, Bandzoogle, or Squarespace to set up a store on your website, where fans can purchase digital downloads, albums, or merchandise.

Integrate a mailing list sign-up to keep fans informed about new releases, exclusive offers, and concerts.

Offer discounts or bundles on your website for fans who purchase multiple items (e.g., an album and a T-shirt).

Leverage Email Marketing

Building an **email list** allows you to engage with your most dedicated fans directly. Email marketing is an effective way to announce new releases, offer exclusive content, and remind fans about upcoming sales or events. Use platforms like Mailchimp or ConvertKit to manage your email campaigns.

Offer free content (such as a free download or exclusive behind-the-scenes content) in exchange for signing up for your mailing list.

Send personalized recommendations, sneak peeks, and exclusive discounts to your subscribers.

Bundle Music with Merchandise

To increase sales and engage fans, consider bundling your music with **merchandise** like T-shirts, posters, or signed physical copies. Merchandise helps you diversify your revenue streams and provides fans with something tangible to represent their support.

Offer special **pre-order bundles** that include digital downloads and exclusive merch.

Create limited-edition bundles to create urgency and exclusivity.

Run Promotions and Discounts

Running **promotions and discounts** for a limited time can encourage fans to purchase your songs. Use holidays, special events, or anniversaries of releases as an opportunity to offer discounted prices or bundles.

Offer a **limited-time discount** on your new album for the first week after its release.

Run a **"pay-what-you-want"** campaign, giving fans the option to contribute more if they want to support your work further.

UTILIZE YOUTUBE AND Streaming to Drive Sales

While streaming platforms like Spotify and YouTube don't sell songs directly, they can drive traffic to your sales pages. Promote your songs on these platforms and include **direct links** to your Bandcamp, website, or digital storefront in the descriptions of your videos or songs.

Use YouTube's description section and pinned comments to direct viewers to purchase your music.

Add Spotify links to your Instagram Stories, encouraging fans to stream and then purchase the song if they enjoy it.

Building an Audience for Your Music: Growing Your Fanbase and Expanding Your Reach

Building an audience for your music is one of the most crucial aspects of becoming a successful artist. Whether you're an independent musician starting out or a more established artist looking to grow, expanding your fanbase requires a combination of strategic marketing, consistent engagement, and leveraging various platforms to connect with potential listeners. A loyal audience not only supports your music but also helps spread the word, leading to organic growth and long-term success. In this chapter, we'll explore how to effectively build an audience for your music, create a lasting connection with fans, and increase your visibility in a crowded music industry.

1. Define Your Target Audience

Before you can start growing your fanbase, it's essential to define your **target audience**. Who are the people most likely to connect with your music? Understanding your audience allows you to tailor your marketing efforts and focus on the platforms, messaging, and content that will resonate with them.

- **Identify your genre and niche**: Determine what genre your music fits into and how it aligns with your artistic vision. Knowing your genre helps you identify the type of audience most likely to enjoy your music—whether it's pop, rock, hip-hop, folk, or another genre.
- **Analyze your influences**: Look at artists or bands that influence your music and examine their fanbases. Where do they engage with their audience? What platforms do they use? Learning from successful artists in your genre can give you insights into where and how to find your audience.
- **Understand your audience's preferences**: Think about the lifestyle, interests, and preferences of your ideal fans. Are they likely to engage on social media platforms like Instagram and TikTok, or are they more inclined to discover music on streaming services like Spotify and Apple Music? Understanding their behavior helps you reach them effectively.

2. Leverage Social Media for Growth

Social media is one of the most powerful tools for building an audience in today's digital age. Platforms like **Instagram**, **TikTok**, **YouTube**, and **Twitter** offer endless opportunities to connect with potential fans, promote your music, and grow your online presence.

Instagram:

Share consistent content: Post regularly to keep your audience engaged. Share photos, videos, and stories that give insight into your creative process, performances, and personal life.

Use hashtags: Use relevant hashtags to make your posts discoverable by people who aren't following you yet. For example, if you're releasing a new single, use hashtags related to your genre, mood, or style of music.

Engage with followers: Respond to comments and messages, and show appreciation for your fans. This interaction helps build a personal connection and makes your audience feel valued.

TikTok:

- **Create viral content**: TikTok is known for its short, viral video format, making it a great platform to share clips of your songs, performance snippets, or behind-the-scenes moments. TikTok's algorithm can expose your music to millions of new listeners quickly.
- **Participate in trends**: Engage with TikTok trends and challenges by incorporating your music into them. You can also create your own challenge around one of your songs, encouraging others to participate and share.

YouTube:

- **Post music videos and live performances**: YouTube is ideal for sharing music videos, acoustic performances, and even lyric videos. Consistently uploading content helps build your channel's presence and attracts new subscribers.
- **Engage with viewers**: Respond to comments and encourage discussions on your videos. The more interaction your videos get, the more likely they are to be recommended to others.

Twitter:

- **Engage in conversations**: Twitter is great for engaging in real-time conversations about music, trends, and your creative process. Participate in discussions related to your genre and interact with fans directly.
- **Promote new releases**: Use Twitter to announce new music, live performances, and important updates, and include links to where fans can listen or buy your songs.

3. Build a Strong Online Presence

Beyond social media, your overall **online presence** should be consistent and professional. This includes having a website, engaging on streaming platforms, and maintaining an email list.

Website:

- **Create a professional website**: Your website serves as the central hub for your music and brand. Include a biography, music releases, tour dates, and a store where fans can buy your music or merchandise. A well-designed website reinforces your credibility and makes it easy for new listeners to find information about you.
- **Offer exclusive content**: Use your website to offer exclusive content, such as unreleased songs, behind-the-scenes videos, or early access to new music. This gives fans a reason to visit your site regularly.

Streaming Platforms:

- **Maximize your streaming presence**: Platforms like **Spotify**, **Apple Music**, and **SoundCloud** are essential for reaching new listeners. Ensure that your music is properly tagged and included in relevant playlists.
- **Submit to playlists**: Getting your music featured in playlists, especially on Spotify, can significantly boost your visibility. Submit your songs to curators and editors to increase your chances of being featured.
- **Track your analytics**: Use the data from streaming platforms to understand where your listeners are coming from, what songs resonate most, and how to adjust your marketing strategy.

Email List:

- **Build and maintain an email list**: An email list allows you to communicate directly with your most loyal fans. Offer incentives such as free downloads or early access to new music to encourage fans to sign up.
- **Send regular updates**: Use email marketing to announce new releases, tour dates, or exclusive offers. Unlike social media, where algorithms may limit your reach, emails land directly in your fans' inboxes.

4. Perform Live and Engage with Local Communities

Performing live is a powerful way to build a dedicated fanbase, especially at the local level. Live shows allow potential fans to experience your music in a personal and immersive setting.

- **Play local gigs**: Start by performing at local venues, open mics, or festivals. Building a strong local fanbase can serve as the foundation for broader regional and national growth.
- **Collaborate with other artists**: Perform with other local musicians or bands to tap into their fanbases and introduce your music to new listeners.
- **Engage with fans at shows**: After performances, take time to meet fans, sign merchandise, and collect email addresses. Personal interactions at live shows help strengthen the connection between you and your audience.
- **Livestream performances**: If you're unable to perform live in person, consider live streaming your performances on platforms like Instagram Live, Facebook Live, or YouTube. Livestreams allow you to reach a global audience and build a fanbase beyond your local area.

---

5. COLLABORATE WITH Other Artists and Influencers

Collaboration is one of the most effective ways to build your audience by tapping into other artists' or influencers' fanbases.

- **Collaborate with fellow musicians**: Whether it's recording a song together, performing a duet, or hosting a joint live stream, collaborating with other artists can introduce you to their audience and vice versa.
- **Work with influencers**: Music influencers on platforms like TikTok or Instagram can help you reach a wider audience. Partner with influencers who align with your brand and have a fanbase that matches your target audience.
- **Create remix or cover challenges**: Encourage other musicians and influencers to remix or cover your songs. These challenges can go viral and expose your music to new listeners, especially if they participate in large numbers.

6. Engage with Your Audience Regularly

Building an audience isn't just about getting listeners—it's about keeping them engaged and turning them into loyal fans. Consistent engagement is key to maintaining a strong relationship with your audience.

- **Respond to fans**: Reply to comments on social media, messages, and emails. When fans see that you're approachable and care about their feedback, they're more likely to stick around and support your music.

- **Run contests and giveaways**: Host contests or giveaways where fans can win exclusive content, merchandise, or concert tickets. These contests help build excitement around your music and incentivize fans to participate.
- **Use polls and Q&As**: Engage with your audience through polls or Q&A sessions on social media. Ask for their input on song ideas, album art, or which songs to perform at shows. This helps your fans feel involved in your creative process and builds a deeper connection.
- **Share personal stories**: Let your fans get to know you beyond the music. Share stories about your life, the inspiration behind your songs, or the challenges you've faced as an artist. Personal storytelling helps humanize you and creates an emotional connection with your audience.

7. Utilize Paid Advertising

While organic growth is important, using **paid advertising** can give your music a boost, especially when promoting new releases or building awareness.

- **Run ads on social media**: Platforms like Facebook, Instagram, and TikTok allow you to create targeted ads that reach potential fans based on their interests, location, and behavior. Promote your new single, album, or music video to attract listeners who are likely to enjoy your music.
- **Boost posts**: Many social media platforms allow you to **boost posts**, increasing their visibility. Boosting posts can help you reach a larger audience than your organic reach, especially when announcing a new release or live show.
- **YouTube ads**: Use YouTube's ad platform to promote your music videos. These ads can be targeted based on user interests and demographics, helping you reach people who are more likely to enjoy your music.

8. Consistency is Key

Building an audience for your music is a marathon, not a sprint. It takes time, effort, and consistent engagement to grow your fanbase.

- **Keep releasing new music**: Consistent releases help keep your audience engaged and excited. Whether it's a single, EP, or full-length album, releasing new music regularly ensures that fans stay connected to your artistic journey.
- **Post regularly on social media**: Consistency on social media is essential for staying visible and building relationships with fans. Stick to a posting schedule that fits your lifestyle and ensures that you're maintaining regular communication with your audience.

Building an audience for your music requires a combination of strategic promotion, authentic engagement, and consistent content creation. By defining your target audience, leveraging social media, performing live, collaborating with other artists, and using both organic and paid marketing tactics, you can grow your fanbase and create a loyal following for your music. Remember, it's not just about the numbers—it's about building meaningful connections with your listeners and turning casual fans into dedicated supporters who will follow your journey and share your music with the world.

Networking in the Music Industry: Building Relationships to Advance Your Career

Networking is an essential part of any career, but it's especially critical in the music industry, where relationships and connections often play a key role in opening doors and creating opportunities. From meeting potential collaborators and producers to securing live gigs or landing a record deal, networking helps you build the relationships that can take your music career to the next level. However, effective networking is more than just handing out business cards or cold emailing people—it's about creating genuine, lasting connections with others in the industry. In this chapter, we'll explore how to effectively network in the music industry, build relationships with key players, and use your connections to advance your career.

1. The Importance of Networking in the Music Industry

In the music industry, talent and hard work are essential, but building relationships is often just as important. Networking allows you to:

- **Access Opportunities**: Many opportunities in the music industry—whether it's a collaboration, live performance, or record deal—come through personal connections. Networking helps you get your foot in the door and opens up possibilities that you might not have access to otherwise.
- **Gain Industry Knowledge**: Networking with other musicians, producers, promoters, and industry professionals gives you valuable insights into how the industry works. These relationships help you stay informed about trends, events, and best practices that can influence your career decisions.
- **Build Your Reputation**: The more you connect with others in the industry, the more your reputation grows. Being known as a reliable, talented, and professional artist can lead to recommendations and referrals that help grow your career.
- **Collaborate and Grow Creatively**: Networking is also about finding creative partners who can enhance your music. Collaborating with other artists, songwriters, and producers can expand your musical horizons and lead to new artistic directions.

2. Where to Network in the Music Industry

There are various places where you can build your network, from online platforms to in-person events. Each offers unique opportunities for connecting with industry professionals and fellow musicians.

Industry Conferences and Festivals

Music industry conferences, festivals, and events provide invaluable networking opportunities. These gatherings are filled with musicians, producers, booking agents, managers, and label representatives. Attending industry events helps you meet people face-to-face and make personal connections.

Examples: Events like **SXSW (South by Southwest)**, **MIDEM**, **ASCAP Expo**, and **NAMM** bring together music industry professionals from around the world. These events often include panels, showcases, and networking mixers where you can connect with key players in the industry.

Strategies: Prepare for these events by researching the attendees or speakers you want to meet. Have business cards, demo links, or social media information ready to share, but remember to focus on building genuine relationships rather than just self-promotion.

Local Music Venues and Open Mics

If you're just starting out, local music venues, open mics, and artist showcases are great places to meet other musicians, promoters, and talent bookers. Playing gigs or attending local shows helps you become part of the local music community and introduces you to people who can support your career.

Strategies: Attend local music events regularly, even when you're not performing. Talk to the venue staff, the sound engineers, and other performers. Building relationships with people behind the scenes can help you secure future gigs or collaborations.

Music Workshops and Classes

Music workshops, masterclasses, and courses provide both education and networking opportunities. Whether it's a songwriting workshop, production class, or artist development seminar, these events are a chance to connect with other musicians and industry professionals who share your interests.

Strategies: Engage actively in these learning environments, participate in discussions, and be open to sharing your experiences. Follow up with the people you meet after the event, especially if you feel a potential connection for collaboration or mentorship.

Social Media and Online Platforms

The internet has made networking in the music industry more accessible than ever. Social media platforms like **Instagram**, **TikTok**, **Twitter**, and **LinkedIn** provide opportunities to connect with other musicians, producers, and industry insiders. These platforms can help you build relationships globally, regardless of your location.

Strategies:

Instagram: Engage with other musicians by liking, commenting, and sharing their content. Direct messaging can lead to more personal conversations and potential collaborations.

Twitter: Use Twitter to join industry conversations, share insights, and connect with people in real-time. Follow artists, managers, and industry leaders to stay in the loop.

LinkedIn: Use LinkedIn for professional networking with industry executives, label representatives, and managers. Keep your profile up to date and connect with people you've met at events or through mutual contacts.

Music Networking Websites

Dedicated music networking platforms such as **SoundBetter, ReverbNation, Indaba Music**, and **Vampr** are designed to connect musicians, producers, and industry professionals. These platforms help you find collaborators, hire producers or session musicians, and connect with other industry figures.

- **Strategies**: Create a professional profile that highlights your skills, experience, and music. Use these platforms to offer your services (e.g., as a songwriter or session musician) and to reach out to potential collaborators.

3. How to Build Genuine Relationships

Networking is most effective when it's about building genuine, mutually beneficial relationships, not just seeking out what others can do for you. Authenticity is key when establishing connections in the music industry.

Be Genuine and Interested

People can tell when you're only connecting with them for personal gain. Instead of focusing on what others can do for you, take a genuine interest in their work, career, and experiences. Ask about their projects, offer your insights or advice, and show support for their music or work.

Offer Value

Networking is a two-way street, and offering value to others is a great way to build strong relationships. Whether it's offering to collaborate on a project, providing helpful feedback, or sharing resources, showing that you're willing to help others will make them more inclined to support you in return.

Be Patient and Consistent

Building strong relationships takes time, so be patient and consistent. Don't expect immediate results from networking interactions. Stay in touch with the people you meet by following up after events or keeping the conversation going online. Consistent engagement over time helps develop trust and familiarity.

Focus on Long-Term Relationships

Aim to build long-term relationships rather than focusing on short-term gains. When you nurture a relationship over time, opportunities tend to arise naturally. Networking isn't about trying to close deals on the spot—it's about laying the foundation for future collaborations and opportunities.

---

4. FOLLOW-UP AND MAINTAIN Connections

Networking doesn't end when you make a connection—**following up** and maintaining relationships is equally important. Staying in touch with the people you meet keeps you on their radar and reinforces the connection.

Follow Up After Events

After meeting someone at an event, be sure to follow up within a few days. Send a polite email or message thanking them for the conversation and expressing interest in staying in touch. You can also remind them of something you discussed to personalize the message.

Keep in Touch

Regularly check in with your contacts to maintain the relationship. This can be as simple as sending a message to congratulate them on a recent achievement, sharing an interesting article related to their work, or offering to grab coffee or meet up at a future event.

Use Social Media to Stay Engaged

Stay engaged with your contacts by interacting with them on social media. Comment on their posts, share their music, and show support for their projects. Social media offers an easy way to maintain a relationship without constant direct communication.

Share Your Own Updates

As you progress in your music career, keep your contacts informed of your milestones, such as releasing new music, booking significant gigs, or collaborating with other artists. This keeps the door open for future opportunities and reminds people of your active presence in the industry.

5. Collaborate and Co-Create

Collaboration is one of the best ways to expand your network in the music industry. Working with other musicians, producers, songwriters, or visual artists allows you to combine your skills and creativity, leading to stronger music and broader exposure.

- **Co-writing songs**: Collaborating with other songwriters can help you create new music and expand your reach, as you'll be exposed to each other's fanbases.
- **Collaborating on performances**: Performing live with other artists or bands can introduce you to their fans and vice versa. Joint gigs and tours can also lead to future collaborations and networking opportunities.
- **Creative partnerships**: Partnering with visual artists, photographers, or videographers can help you create unique content that enhances your brand and promotes your music. These partnerships also expose your music to new audiences, particularly through social media.

6. Networking with Industry Professionals

Connecting with **music industry professionals**, such as managers, producers, booking agents, and label representatives, can help you advance your career. However, it's important to approach these relationships professionally and respectfully.

Do Your Research

Before approaching industry professionals, research their background and experience. Knowing what projects they've worked on or which artists they represent can help you tailor your approach and demonstrate that you're genuinely interested in working with them.

Be Professional

When reaching out to industry professionals, always be polite, respectful, and concise. Whether it's an email, social media message, or in-person introduction, keep your communication clear and to the point. Respect their time and avoid being overly pushy or demanding.

Offer a Strong Value Proposition

When pitching your music or discussing potential collaboration with industry professionals, focus on what you bring to the table. Highlight your achievements, unique qualities, and vision, and explain why you believe the collaboration would be mutually beneficial.

7. Attend Virtual Networking Events

In the age of remote work and digital communication, **virtual networking events** have become more common. Many conferences, workshops, and industry events now offer online networking opportunities, allowing you to connect with people from around the world without leaving home.

- **Attend virtual panels or webinars**: Participate in online industry events where you can learn from experts and meet other attendees.
- **Join virtual meetups**: Many industry organizations, music schools, or communities host virtual networking meetups. These events are great for meeting people in a more relaxed, digital environment.

Networking in the music industry is essential for building relationships, accessing opportunities, and advancing your career. By attending industry events, engaging online, collaborating with other artists, and maintaining professional relationships, you can expand your network and build a supportive community around your music. Remember that networking is about creating genuine connections—focus on building long-term relationships and offering value to others, and the opportunities will follow. With the right approach, networking can open doors to collaborations, gigs, and career-defining moments in the music industry.

Performing Your Songs Live: Captivating Audiences and Building Your Stage Presence

Performing your songs live is one of the most exciting and rewarding aspects of being a musician. It gives you the opportunity to showcase your music, connect with your audience on a personal level, and build your fanbase. However, live performance also comes with its challenges, including stage fright, technical issues, and the need to engage and captivate your audience from the first note to the last. Whether you're performing in a small local venue or on a larger stage, mastering the art of live performance is crucial to building your music career. In this chapter, we'll explore the key elements of performing live, from preparation to stage presence, and offer tips on how to deliver an unforgettable show.

1. Preparing for Your Live Performance

A successful live performance begins long before you step onto the stage. Proper preparation ensures that you feel confident and ready to give your best performance, while also allowing you to focus on connecting with your audience.

Rehearse, Rehearse, Rehearse

The foundation of any great live performance is solid rehearsal. Rehearsing not only helps you perfect your songs but also builds your confidence so that you're comfortable performing in front of an audience.

- **Full-band rehearsal**: If you're performing with a band, make sure to schedule regular rehearsals where you practice both individual parts and playing together as a group. Pay attention to transitions between songs, dynamics, and timing, so your set flows smoothly.
- **Practice like it's a show**: During rehearsal, simulate a live performance as closely as possible. Run through your setlist in order, practice talking to the audience between songs, and work on your stage movement and presence. This helps you feel more comfortable on stage and ensures that your performance feels natural.

Create a Compelling Setlist

A well-structured setlist is key to keeping your audience engaged throughout your performance. Think about how you want the energy of your show to flow, balancing high-energy songs with slower or more intimate moments.

Start strong: Open your set with a powerful song that grabs the audience's attention and sets the tone for the rest of the performance.

Mix tempos and moods: Vary the pace of your set to keep the audience engaged. Follow up an energetic song with a slower one to give your listeners a breather, then pick the energy back up.

Save a standout for last: End your set with one of your strongest or most popular songs. A memorable closing song leaves a lasting impression on the audience and may prompt an encore.

Know the Venue and Equipment

Familiarize yourself with the venue and the technical aspects of your performance ahead of time. Knowing what to expect will help you avoid surprises and ensure that your performance goes smoothly.

- **Visit the venue**: If possible, visit the venue before your show to get a feel for the stage, the sound system, and the layout. Understanding the space will help you plan how to move around on stage and interact with the audience.
- **Check your equipment**: Whether you're using your own gear or relying on the venue's equipment, make sure everything is in working order. Test your instruments, microphones, and effects pedals, and ensure you have backup cables, strings, and batteries on hand.
- **Soundcheck**: Arrive early for a soundcheck to ensure that your levels are balanced and that you're comfortable with the mix. Use this time to make sure you can hear yourself clearly on stage and communicate any preferences to the sound engineer.

2. Overcoming Stage Fright

Even experienced performers sometimes struggle with **stage fright** or nerves before a show. While some nervousness is normal, learning how to manage it is key to delivering a confident performance.

Mental Preparation

Preparing mentally for your performance is just as important as rehearsing your songs. Developing a positive mindset can help you overcome stage fright and stay focused during the show.

- **Visualize success**: Before stepping on stage, take a moment to visualize a successful performance. Picture yourself performing confidently and imagine the audience enjoying your music. This can help reduce anxiety and increase your confidence.
- **Breathe deeply**: Deep breathing exercises can help calm your nerves. Take slow, deep breaths before you go on stage to reduce stress and help you focus on the performance.
- **Positive self-talk**: Replace any negative thoughts with positive affirmations. Remind yourself that you've prepared for this moment, and that the audience is there to enjoy your music. Focusing on your excitement about performing can help shift your mindset away from fear.

EMBRACE THE ENERGY

Instead of trying to eliminate stage fright completely, learn to channel that nervous energy into your performance. A little adrenaline can enhance your stage presence, giving you more energy and intensity on stage.

Connect with the audience: Focus on engaging with your audience rather than worrying about how you're being perceived. Smile, make eye contact, and interact with the crowd—this helps shift your focus from internal anxieties to the external experience of performing.

Use your nervous energy: Nervous energy can give your performance a boost of intensity. Use that energy to move around the stage, engage with your bandmates, and bring excitement to your songs.

3. Building Stage Presence

Your **stage presence**—the way you command attention and connect with the audience—plays a huge role in how memorable your performance is. Even if your music is technically flawless, an engaging stage presence can take your live show to the next level.

Engage with the Audience

The most successful live performers make their audience feel like they're part of the experience. Engaging with the crowd helps build a connection that makes the performance more personal and memorable.

- **Make eye contact**: Looking out into the audience and making eye contact with individuals creates a sense of connection. It shows that you're present in the moment and that you care about interacting with your listeners.
- **Move around the stage**: Don't stay glued to one spot. Move around the stage to create a dynamic performance. Engage with your bandmates, use different areas of the stage, and interact with the audience from different angles.
- **Speak to the crowd**: Between songs, take the time to talk to your audience. Share the story behind a song, thank them for coming, or acknowledge something happening in the room. These moments of conversation make the performance feel more intimate and personal.

Own the Stage

Confidence is key when it comes to commanding the stage. Even if you're feeling nervous, acting confident can help you project energy and keep the audience's attention.

Body language matters: Your body language communicates a lot to the audience. Stand tall, avoid looking down, and use open, expansive gestures to convey confidence.

Be expressive: Use your facial expressions and body movements to enhance the emotional impact of your songs. Whether you're singing a heartfelt ballad or an upbeat anthem, show your audience how you feel through your physical presence.

Practice stage movement: If you're unsure how to move on stage, practice during rehearsal. Work on making your movements feel natural and in sync with the music. Over time, you'll develop a performance style that suits your personality and music.

4. Handling Technical Issues and Mistakes

Even the most prepared performers can encounter technical issues or make mistakes during a live show. The key is learning how to handle these moments gracefully and keep the performance going.

Stay Calm and Composed

When something goes wrong—whether it's a technical glitch, a missed note, or an unexpected audience reaction—stay calm and composed. Most audiences won't notice small mistakes unless you draw attention to them, so continue playing confidently.

- **Keep playing**: If you or a bandmate makes a mistake, keep playing through it. A slight misstep won't ruin the show, and recovering quickly helps maintain the flow of the performance.

- **Acknowledge technical issues if necessary**: If there's a significant technical problem, such as a microphone failure or an instrument cutting out, acknowledge it with humor or a brief explanation. Stay positive and use the moment to engage with the audience while the issue is being resolved.

Have a Backup Plan

Being prepared for technical issues can help you handle them more smoothly.

- **Bring backups**: Always bring backup equipment, such as extra strings, picks, cables, or batteries. If you're using electronics, have a backup plan for going acoustic in case something malfunctions.
- **Communicate with your sound engineer**: Establish clear communication with the sound engineer before the show. If something goes wrong during the performance, they'll be more likely to help you resolve the issue quickly if you've built a good rapport.

5. Interacting with Your Fans after the Show

Your connection with the audience doesn't have to end when the performance does. Taking time to interact with fans after the show helps build a loyal fanbase and leaves a lasting positive impression.

Meet and Greet

After your performance, take time to meet your fans, sign merchandise, or take photos. These interactions help create personal connections and make your fans feel appreciated.

Show gratitude: Thank your audience for coming to the show and supporting your music. Genuine appreciation goes a long way in building long-term relationships with your fans.

Collect fan information: If possible, collect email addresses or encourage fans to follow you on social media. Building an email list or growing your social media following helps you stay in touch with fans after the show and keep them informed about future performances or releases.

Sustaining Creativity in Songwriting: Keeping the Inspiration Alive

Songwriting is a deeply creative process, but like any form of artistic expression, it's not always easy to keep the inspiration flowing. Whether you're a seasoned songwriter or just starting out, there will inevitably be times when you feel stuck or uninspired. The key to a long and successful songwriting career is learning how to **sustain creativity** over the long term, even when the ideas don't seem to come as easily. In this chapter, we'll explore ways to keep your creative spark alive, overcome writer's block, and continually find new sources of inspiration.

1. Embrace a Creative Routine

Creativity often thrives on structure. While spontaneity can lead to great ideas, having a regular routine for your songwriting helps you stay productive even when inspiration isn't striking. By making songwriting a consistent habit, you train yourself to be creative on demand rather than waiting for the perfect moment.

Set Aside Time for Songwriting

One of the most effective ways to sustain creativity is to make songwriting part of your daily or weekly routine. Set aside dedicated time to write, whether it's an hour a day or a few sessions each week. This creates a **creative rhythm** that keeps you engaged with your music regularly, even when you don't feel inspired.

- **Consistency matters**: Just like any skill, songwriting improves with practice. By making time for it regularly, you're more likely to stay sharp and inspired.
- **Treat it like a job**: Many professional songwriters treat their work like a 9-to-5 job, showing up every day to write, whether they feel inspired or not. The key is to write consistently, knowing that not every session will produce a masterpiece, but every session is valuable practice.

Warm Up Before Writing

Before diving into a songwriting session, spend a few minutes **warming up** your creative muscles. Just as athletes stretch before a workout, songwriters can benefit from creative warm-up exercises.

- **Freewriting**: Spend 10 minutes writing whatever comes to mind without worrying about structure, grammar, or making sense. This can help clear mental clutter and open your mind to new ideas.
- **Lyric prompts**: Use a word or phrase as a prompt to generate new ideas. Write a few lines of lyrics based on that prompt, even if it's unrelated to what you're working on.
- **Play an instrument**: If you're feeling stuck, pick up an instrument and play around with different chord progressions, melodies, or rhythms. Sometimes the physical act of playing can lead to new ideas.

2. Seek Inspiration from New Sources

Creativity often stagnates when you rely on the same sources of inspiration. To keep your songwriting fresh, it's important to seek out new experiences, perspectives, and creative stimuli.

Listen to Different Genres

One of the easiest ways to spark new ideas is to listen to music outside your usual genre. Exploring different styles and artists can introduce you to new chord progressions, rhythms, and lyrical themes that you may not have considered before.

- **Cross-genre inspiration**: If you typically write pop songs, try listening to jazz, classical, or hip-hop for inspiration. You might discover a unique approach to melody or rhythm that you can incorporate into your own style.
- **Study the greats**: Analyze the work of master songwriters from different genres, such as Bob Dylan for storytelling, Stevie Wonder for chord progressions, or Joni Mitchell for lyrical complexity. Learning from different songwriters can help expand your creative toolbox.

Step Outside of Music

Inspiration doesn't always have to come from other songs. Many songwriters find creative fuel in other forms of art, such as literature, films, visual art, or personal experiences.

- **Read poetry or literature**: Poets and authors often use language in creative ways that can inspire your lyrics. Reading a poem or a novel can spark an idea for a theme, a lyric, or even the structure of a song.
- **Watch films**: Films are a rich source of inspiration for storytelling, mood, and emotion. Pay attention to the way a film's plot develops or how the soundtrack enhances its emotional impact. Use these elements to inspire your own songwriting.
- **Engage with visual art**: Paintings, sculptures, and photography can evoke emotions, stories, or images that lead to songwriting ideas. Visit a gallery or browse artwork online and see what feelings or stories the images inspire.

Explore Personal Experiences

Songwriting often draws from personal experiences, emotions, and memories. If you're feeling creatively blocked, take time to reflect on your own life and use those experiences as the foundation for your songs.

- **Journal your thoughts**: Keeping a journal of your thoughts, feelings, and experiences can provide a wealth of material for songwriting. Write about what's happening in your life, how you're feeling, and any challenges you're facing. These raw emotions often translate into powerful lyrics.
- **Write about others**: Songwriting doesn't always have to be autobiographical. Try writing from the perspective of someone else—a character in a story, a friend, or even a historical figure. This can open up new narrative possibilities and creative directions.

3. Break the Rules and Experiment

Creativity often comes from **breaking free** of the rules and expectations that typically govern songwriting. Don't be afraid to experiment with your process, try new techniques, and step outside of your comfort zone.

Play with Song Structure

Most popular songs follow familiar structures, such as verse-chorus-verse or AABA. While these structures work for a reason, stepping outside of them can lead to more interesting and creative results.

- **Try a new structure**: Experiment with writing a song that doesn't follow a traditional structure. For example, try writing a song with no chorus, or one that builds continuously without repeating sections. This can lead to unique songs that stand out from the norm.
- **Combine genres**: Mix elements from different musical genres to create something new. Combining pop melodies with jazz harmonies, or blending rock instrumentation with electronic beats, can result in a fresh sound that reflects your diverse influences.

Change Your Writing Environment

Sometimes a change in environment is all it takes to unlock creativity. If you always write in the same place, try moving to a different location to see if it sparks new ideas.

- **Write outside**: If you're used to writing in a studio or at home, try taking your guitar or notebook to a park, beach, or coffee shop. The change of scenery can refresh your perspective and stimulate creativity.
- **Travel**: Traveling to a new city, country, or even a different part of your own town can expose you to new experiences, cultures, and ideas that can inspire your songwriting.

Use New Instruments or Tools

If you typically write with the same instrument or tool, switching things up can bring new ideas to the surface.

- **Try a different instrument**: If you usually write on guitar, try switching to piano, or vice versa. Using a different instrument can inspire new melodies, chords, and arrangements that you might not have discovered otherwise.

- **Experiment with technology**: Use digital tools like loop pedals, drum machines, or software like Ableton or Logic Pro to create new sounds and textures. Experimenting with different production techniques can open up new creative possibilities.

4. Collaborate with Other Songwriters

Collaborating with other songwriters can inject new energy into your songwriting process and push you to explore ideas you might not have considered on your own. Working with someone else can break down creative barriers and open up new directions for your music.

Co-Writing

Co-writing with another songwriter allows you to blend your strengths and ideas, often leading to more dynamic and well-rounded songs.

- **Bring in a fresh perspective**: A collaborator can offer new ideas for melodies, lyrics, or arrangements that you may not have thought of. They may also suggest changes that improve a song's structure or flow.
- **Learn from each other**: Collaborating allows you to learn from someone else's songwriting process. You can pick up new techniques or approaches that you can apply to your solo work.

Join a Songwriting Group

Joining a **songwriting group** or workshop gives you access to a community of songwriters who can offer feedback, support, and inspiration.

- **Share your work**: Sharing your songs with others in the group gives you valuable feedback and new perspectives on your music. Listening to other people's songs can also inspire your own writing.
- **Set goals together**: Being part of a group often leads to accountability, where you set goals for writing new songs or completing projects. This can help you stay motivated and productive.

---

5. OVERCOME CREATIVE Blocks

It's normal for every songwriter to experience **creative blocks** from time to time. The key to overcoming these blocks is to approach them with patience and persistence.

Take Breaks

Sometimes, the best way to overcome a creative block is to step away from songwriting for a while. Take a break, clear your mind, and allow yourself to return to the process with fresh eyes.

- **Do something unrelated**: Engage in activities that have nothing to do with music—exercise, read a book, cook, or spend time with friends. Often, taking your mind off the problem allows new ideas to come to you naturally.
- **Let ideas percolate**: Creativity doesn't always happen on command. If you're struggling to finish a song, give yourself permission to set it aside and come back to it later. Allow the ideas to develop in the background

while you focus on other things.

Push Through Resistance

At other times, the best way to break through a creative block is to keep writing, even when it feels difficult. By pushing through the resistance, you might discover ideas that you didn't know were there.

- **Write through the block**: Set a timer for 10 or 15 minutes and force yourself to write anything, even if it feels uninspired. The act of writing often leads to breakthroughs, even if you don't feel motivated at the start.
- **Embrace imperfection**: Don't worry about writing the perfect song every time. Allow yourself to write songs that aren't your best—sometimes, these "failed" songs lead to ideas or fragments that become great songs later on.

Sustaining creativity in songwriting requires a combination of routine, experimentation, and openness to new ideas. By embracing a regular songwriting practice, seeking inspiration from different sources, experimenting with new techniques, and collaborating with others, you can keep your creativity alive and continue producing fresh, compelling songs. Remember that creativity ebbs and flows, and it's okay to experience periods of lower inspiration. The important thing is to stay engaged with your craft and be willing to explore new directions when inspiration strikes. With the right mindset and approach, you can sustain your creativity and continue growing as a songwriter throughout your career.

Good luck in your songwriting career.

Andrew

Don't miss out!

Visit the website below and you can sign up to receive emails whenever Andrew Parry publishes a new book. There's no charge and no obligation.

https://books2read.com/r/B-A-FROLC-UJICF

BOOKS 2 READ

Connecting independent readers to independent writers.